The
500
BEST-VALUE
WINES
in the LCBO

2009

The
500
BEST-VALUE
WINES
in the LCBO

~≋ 2009 ≋~

ROD PHILLIPS

whitecap

Whitecap Books is known for its expertise in the cookbook market, and has produced
some of the most innovative and familiar titles found in kitchens across North America.
Visit our website at www.whitecap.ca

The information in this book is true and complete to the best of the author's knowledge. Prices quoted in this book were correct when it went to press but are subject to
change. All recommendations are made without guarantee on the part of the author
or Whitecap Books Ltd. The author and publisher disclaim any liability in connection
with the use of this information.

EDITOR   Julia Aitken
DESIGNER   Grace Partridge
TYPESETTER   Setareh Ashrafologhalai
PROOFREADER   Joan Tetrault

Printed in Canada.

❀

Library and Archives Canada Cataloguing in Publication

Phillips, Roderick
      The 500 best-value wines in the LCBO 2009 / Rod Phillips.

Includes index.
ISBN 978-1-55285-938-4

      1. Wine and wine making. 2. Liquor Control Board of Ontario.
1. Title. II. Title: Five hundred best-value wines in the LCBO 2009.

TP548.P496 2008   641.2'2   C2008-902144-4

The publisher acknowledges the financial support of the Government of Canada
through the Book Publishing Industry Development Program (BPIDP) and the
Province of British Columbia through the Book Publishing Tax Credit.

08 09 10 11 12 5 4 3 2 1

CONTENTS

The Reds

PREFACE

This book shows you the best-value wines from the huge range in LCBO stores throughout Ontario. (And if you're not in Ontario, you'll find many of these wines where you live.) If you tend to buy one wine time after time, this list will help broaden your horizons and, at the same time, minimize the risk in being adventurous. With so many good- to great-value wines on sale at reasonable prices through the LCBO, it's a pity not to take advantage of them.

I tasted nearly all the wines continuously available in the LCBO and Vintages, and the reviews in this book point you to wine styles you'll easily recognize. Each wine is ranked out of five stars (see How I Rated the Wines, page 10) but I encourage you to read the description of each wine. If you don't like red wines that are bold and tannic, even one that I rate as five stars probably won't convert you.

I hope you find this book a useful guide to discovering wines you enjoy. If you try a wine that's not in here but that you think should be included in the next edition, please let me know. You can reach me at rod@rodphillipsonwine.com.

Cheers!

THANKS

I want to thank all the wine agencies and individual wineries, together with their sales and marketing representatives, for providing me with the wines I tasted for this book.

Thanks also to the Liquor Control Board of Ontario (LCBO) for inviting me to the regular tastings of Vintages and General Purchase wines.

Again, it was a pleasure to work with the people at Whitecap Books: Robert McCullough, Taryn Boyd, Julia Aitken, Mauve Pagé, Michelle Mayne, Joan Tetrault, Grace Yaginuma, and Setareh Ashrafologhalai.

WHAT'S NEW IN THE 2009 EDITION?

The most important change in the 2009 edition is the addition of 180 new wines. Of course, I've deleted 180 that were in the 2008 edition to make room for them, so there is a 36 percent turnover. The wines most affected by the changes are whites from California, France, and Ontario, and reds from Australia, California, Chile, France, Italy, and Ontario.

Most of the new wines here are also new to the LCBO, but after re-tasting the liquor board's entire inventory, I included some this year that were excluded from the 2008 edition. Although there is not a great deal of variation from vintage to vintage in most of the LCBO wines, there is some. The ratings of certain wines also changed. There's a new category this year, too: kosher wines.

I've also changed the way I review the wines. I've moved on from descriptions that refer to fruit, berries, spices, and herbs, and focused on the style of each wine: Whether it's a light- or full-bodied wine, whether it's fruity or structured, whether it's tannic or not, whether it has a smooth, tangy, or crisp texture.

After all, that's the way most of us describe the wines we like. We say we prefer red wine that's full bodied and rich, or white that's delicate and crisp. And when we're looking for wine to go with dinner, we think of a heavy red for steak or a lighter white for fish. We don't think in terms of whether a wine has flavours of black plums or raspberries, or has notes of red grapefruit, black pepper, or honey. And we certainly don't say we love wines with flavours of wet stones, smoky tar, or hard-ridden horses—the sort of comparisons loved by some reviewers. You'll find that this book describes wines in the common-sense way most people think of them.

HOW I RATED THE WINES

I tasted not only all the wines listed in this book, but another thousand or so in addition. They represent the wines available in the LCBO General Purchase and the Vintages Essentials lists. As far as I know, this is the first time one person has tasted all these wines in a short period (I did it in a month), and this has given me a unique perspective on the liquor board's inventory.

I tasted the reds at cool room temperature—the way they should be served—and the whites, rosés, and sparkling wines chilled—the way we drink them.

The 500 wines in this book are the ones I consider the best in terms of their intrinsic quality and value. The quality of a wine depends on the complexity of its flavours and texture, and the balance among its various components (fruit, acidity, and tannins). A wine that's very complex and finely balanced scores higher than one with little complexity or poor balance.

All the wines here are good-to-excellent quality, and the five-star rating reflects their value to the consumer. For example, if I gave four stars to a wine that costs $10, I would give a lower rating to a $20 wine of the same quality. At the same time, the value rating is also a guide to quality, because the adjustment for value is generally a matter of only half a star. No wine that garners five stars for quality would be demoted to three-star value simply because it's expensive, and no three-star wine would be awarded five stars just for being inexpensive.

Here's what the star system means:

★ ★ ★ ★ ★   I can't imagine better value. The wine is very complex and very well balanced.

★ ★ ★ ★ ½   Excellent value. The wine is very complex and well balanced.

★ ★ ★ ★   Very good value. The wine is complex and well balanced.

★ ★ ★ ½   Above average value. The wine has fair levels of complexity and balance.

★ ★ ★   Good value. A straightforward and well-made wine.

RATING (*out of five*)

BRAND OR WINERY

GRAPE VARIETY

VINTAGE YEAR

REGION

★ ★ ★ ★ ½   **Cave Spring 'Estate Bottled' Riesling 2006**

VQA BEAMSVILLE BENCH $17.80   (286377)

[Vintages Essential] Beamsville Bench is one of more than a dozen sub-appellations (or sub-regions) that the Niagara Peninsula wine region has been divided into. It might be a bit confusing for consumers, but what's *not* confusing is this only just off-dry Riesling. It delivers delicious, intense flavours on a texture that's brisk, clean, and makes you want to eat. So eat. Pair this with spicy seafood or smoked salmon.

NOTES

....

....

....

....

....

Indicates it is found in the Vintages section, or at a Vintages store.

LCBO PRODUCT CODE

PRICE
(per 750 mL bottle, unless otherwise indicated)

11

ABOUT THE LCBO

The LCBO (Liquor Control Board of Ontario) sells more than 85 percent of the wine purchased in the province. Its wine sales totalled more than $1.4 billion in fiscal year 2007/2008. The other 15 percent was sold by winery retail stores, online suppliers, or importing agents. The LCBO is where most Ontarians shop for wine because it has so many locations and offers the biggest range of imported and Canadian wine in Ontario.

Critics of the LCBO often complain that its wine selection is too limited, but most consumers find it bewilderingly large. So this book guides you to the best values on the General Purchase list, which makes up most of the wines at the LCBO. The others are in Vintages stores or Vintages sections of the LCBO.

It can sometimes be a challenge to locate a particular wine at the LCBO. There are nearly 600 LCBO stores throughout the province, as well as small agencies in isolated localities, but the range of wines available varies widely. The main LCBO stores in major cities carry nearly all the LCBO's wines, while smaller outlets have a much more restricted selection.

If you see a wine in this book that you'd like to try, but discover it's not in your local LCBO, ask the store's Product Consultant for help. These consultants have passed wine knowledge examinations and know the LCBO's inventory well. Or, call the LCBO helpline at 1-800-ONT-LCBO (1-800-668-5226). An agent will tell you the nearest store that carries the wine you're looking for. The search engine on the LCBO website (www.lcbo.com) also enables you to find a wine and identify the LCBO stores that have it.

Bear in mind that the LCBO's inventory changes constantly. New wines are added and others are dropped. Prices change, too, according to currency exchange fluctuations and other factors. The prices in this book were correct when it went to press.

Vintages available also change. You might see a 2004 wine listed here but find that the 2005 vintage is on the LCBO shelf. For the most part, there is relatively little variation among vintages in the wines on the General Purchase list, and it's safe to go with my reviews and ratings even when the vintage is different.

BUYING, SERVING & DRINKING WINE: SOME COMMON QUESTIONS

Are wines sealed with a screw cap poorer quality than wines sealed with a cork?
Not at all. In fact, some of the best-known producers, like Wolf Blass and
Peter Lehmann in Australia, seal all their still wines, including their top
brands, with screw caps. There's still some debate about the use of screw
caps on wines intended for long-term aging, but there's no doubt that
they are excellent for wines meant to be drunk within a few years of being
made—like the wines in this book. Natural corks can contain bacteria
capable of mildly or seriously tainting wine, and it's estimated that
between three and ten percent of bottles are affected this way. Natural
corks can produce variability from bottle to bottle; wines with screw caps
tend to be more consistent. Are screw caps the last word in wine-bottle
closures? Probably not, as experiments continue with other types of seals.

*Are wines in boxes and plastic bottles poorer quality than wines in
glass bottles?*
Many people think only inferior wine is sold in boxes (like Tetra Paks)
and plastic bottles (like PET, a food-grade plastic that does not taint the
contents). You can't generalize about the quality of wine from its packaging; there are plenty of poor wines in glass bottles. In practice, though,
many producers put their lower-quality wines in boxes or plastic. The
only reason excellent wine might not be sold this way is that there's some
question about how long boxes or plastic preserve wine in good condition.
Still, a number of the wines selected for this book, including some that are
highly rated, come in Tetra Paks or PET bottles. The LCBO encourages the
use of Tetra Paks and plastic for environmental reasons because this packaging is much lighter than glass and saves energy in transportation.

Are more expensive wines better than cheaper ones?
In very broad terms, there is often a relationship between quality and
price. High-quality wine demands high-quality grapes (which are often
pricier to grow or buy) and may involve more expenses in production,
such as oak barrels. But although it's not as easy to find a great wine for
less than $10 or $15, this book shows that there are plenty of high-quality
wines at very reasonable prices.

Are wine labels a good guide to what's inside the bottle?

Labels are an important part of marketing wine. Wine is no different from other products in that producers expect consumers will often be drawn to a particular wine by its packaging—and that usually means the label. Labels can be sophisticated (like many expensive and super-premium wines), fun (like most of the animal labels), and even provocative (like the Fat Bastard brand). The fact that all are represented in this book shows that there's no necessary link between the label and quality or value. But beyond projecting an image, labels provide consumers with important information. Depending on where the wine is from, you'll find details of the grape variety (or varieties) in the wine and/or where the grapes were grown. The label also tells you the vintage year, alcohol content, as well as whether the wine is organic or kosher. Some of this information might be on a back label, along with a description of the wine, the production process, or the maker. Bear in mind that any back-label description of the wine is written by the producer in order to promote sales.

Does the serving temperature of wine make any difference?

How you serve wine *does* matter, as the right temperature enhances qualities such as flavour and acidity. Overall, consumers (and too many restaurants) tend to serve white wine too cold and red wine too warm. White wines are refreshing when they're chilled, but most should not be served straight from the fridge. Let white wine stand at room temperature for 15 minutes or so before you serve it. Red wine, on the other hand, should be served cooler than it usually is—especially in restaurants where the wine is stored on shelves in the dining room. Red wine should feel cool in your mouth, and that means cooler than the 20°C of most homes and restaurants in North America. (The guideline of serving red wine "at room temperature" is not very useful now that we have central heating.) If your red wine is too warm, it will feel coarse and flabby and won't have the refreshing quality that makes wine such an ideal partner for food. To cool red wine that's too warm, put it in the fridge for 15 to 20 minutes before serving. Remember, it's better to serve any wine too cool than too warm; it will warm up quite quickly in your glass.

How many different kinds of wine glasses do I need?

Look in wine accessory, kitchen, and even many department stores, and you'll see a wide selection of wine glasses in many different shapes and sizes, often labelled for a specific grape variety. Do you really need one glass for Chardonnay, another for Merlot, another for Pinot Noir? No, you don't. Although the shape and size of the glass can highlight the qualities in wine, you can enjoy nearly all wines from one or two different glasses. In general, people enjoy wine more if it's served in fine glasses than in thick-sided tumblers. Look for glasses that are wider towards the bottom of the bowl, and fill the glass only to the widest point. That gives room for the aromas to collect. And if you're interested in tasting wine as judges and professionals do, buy some ISO (International Organization for Standardization) glasses at a wine accessory store. They're smaller, wide at the bottom, and tapered towards the mouth (like the stylized glasses on the cover of this book), and they bring out the aromas and flavours of wines very well. One style of wine that you should serve in a specific glass is sparkling wine. A tall, slender glass (called a flute) shows off the bubbles to best effect.

Should I let wine "breathe" before I serve it?

There's a common misconception that wine should be opened and left standing to "breathe" for an hour or two before serving. It's based on the fact that most wine is generally improved by being exposed to air for a short time. But simply opening a bottle of wine exposes just a dime-sized surface in the neck of the bottle, and makes no perceptible difference. Pouring the wine into glasses as soon as it's opened airs the wine far more effectively than letting it stand in the bottle for hours. You can also decant wine to expose it to air, and that raises the question . . .

Do I need to decant wine?

There are two reasons to decant wine. The first is to pour the wine off any sediment that may have collected in the bottom of the bottle to make sure it doesn't get into your glass. Of course, this is rarely necessary with wines made for early drinking, like virtually all those in this book. The second reason to decant does apply to the wines here—in fact, it applies to any wine, whether it's red, white, or rosé—and that's to expose wine to some air before you drink it. This is more accurately called "aerating" than "decanting," and it generally improves the aromas, flavours, and texture of the wine, and therefore its overall quality. You needn't buy an expensive decanter (there are many on the market for less than $15), but look for one with a broad mouth and a wide bottom. If you don't have a decanter, pour the wine into a clean bottle then back into the original bottle a couple of times.

What do I do with leftover wine?

Opened wine lasts longer if you store it in the fridge and longer still if you minimize its exposure to air. Just re-corking or screwing the cap back on a half-finished bottle leaves the wine exposed to a lot of air, so it's better to pour leftover wine into a smaller container, like a clean half-bottle. Refrigerated like this, leftover wine should be good for at least two or three days. There are also all manner of gadgets out there for preserving wine, such as pumps and inert-gas sprays, found at specialty wine stores and kitchen shops—some are more effective than others. If you have leftover sparkling wine, use the same resealer as you'd use for carbonated soft drinks.

Does wine improve with age? Should I have a wine cellar?

While some wines age well, the great bulk of the world's wine is made for drinking as soon as it's released for sale. It will not improve with age. Only a few of the wines in this book will, and this is mentioned in the specific reviews. Although most consumers buy wine as they need it, there's no reason why you shouldn't keep a number of bottles on hand for emergencies. For that purpose, you don't need a proper cellar with controlled temperature and humidity, but your wine will keep best if it's in a dark, cool place (ideally between 10ºc and 18ºc). The corner of a basement, a closet, the space under stairs—all might be suitable. However storing wine on a kitchen counter, where it's exposed to light and heat, is not. Wine kept in too-warm conditions develops a "stewed" flavour. If you do want to store a few dozen or more bottles of wine so that they improve over a longer term, check the internet or a wine accessory store for information on wine cabinets or instructions for building a wine cellar.

MATCHING WINE & FOOD

Matching food with wine is not nearly as difficult as many people think. There are a few basic guidelines that help you choose a pairing that does what it should: enhance your enjoyment of both the food and the wine. What you want to avoid is a situation where one overwhelms or interferes with your enjoyment of the other. For example, a full-flavoured wine will smother delicate food, and very sweet food can make wine taste sour.

Matching wine and food is fun, and if you follow a few simple guidelines, you won't go far wrong. Some pairings will seem better than others, but none of them should be disastrous. Most of the reviews in this book include a possible food match, but don't take these too literally. Each suggestion represents a style. A wine that goes with beef will team well with lamb, and one that pairs with chicken will probably complement turkey or pork.

GUIDELINES FOR WHITE & RED WINE

- Match heavier dishes (like red meat and hearty meat or vegetable stews) with medium- to full-bodied wines, and lighter dishes (like salads and white fish) with light- to medium-bodied wines. The weight of food often comes from sauces: White fish alone is light, but a cream sauce makes it heavier.

- Focus on the dominant flavours of the entire dish, not just the main item. Unseasoned roast chicken tastes mild but chicken in a rich, piquant tomato sauce has full and spicy flavours.

- Herbs and spices give richness and complexity to food. Barbecued pork has more flavour than unseasoned pork, for example, and a wine that pairs well with richer, more complex food will match it better.

- Focus on the style of the wine, not just its colour. For the purpose of matching food, a full-bodied, rich Chardonnay might have more in common with a red wine than with a light-bodied, delicate white.

FOOD MATCHES FOR WHITE & RED WINE

- Fish and seafood pair well with Sauvignon Blanc, especially when the dish is served with fresh lemon juice. Some crisp Pinot Grigios/Pinot Gris, dry Rieslings, and unoaked Chardonnays also go well.

- Sushi made with raw fish and eaten with ginger and wasabi pairs well with fruity Pinot Grigios/Pinot Gris, off-dry Rieslings, and Gewürztraminers.

- Smoked fish and smoked seafood go well with off-dry Rieslings or off-dry Gewürztraminers.

- Heavier fish and seafood dishes, like fish or mussels in a cream sauce, seared scallops, or lobster with melted butter, go well with heavier Chardonnays, especially oaked versions.

- Salmon and tuna, either grilled or seared, go well with lighter Pinot Noirs or oaked Chardonnays.

- Chicken, turkey, veal, and pork pair well with oaked Chardonnay if the dish is fairly simple and is not dominated by other flavours. Chicken and turkey complement red wines such as Gamay, Pinot Noir, lighter-styled Merlot and Shiraz/Syrah, and dry rosé. Pork and dry Riesling work very well together.

- Beef, lamb, and red meat stews go well with full-bodied red wines, such as Cabernet Sauvignon, Merlot, Malbec, Shiraz/Syrah, Carmenère, and red blends, especially Bordeaux blends such as Cabernet/Merlot.

- Italian food featuring tomatoes, like pizza and some pasta sauces, is acidic and goes well with red wines with higher acidity (a feature of many Italian wines). Wine made from the Sangiovese grape (such as Chianti) often fits the bill, as do most red wines in this book described as having a crisp, tangy, or refreshing texture.

- Spicy dishes, such as much Asian cuisine, go well with sparkling or a light and fruity wine. Try off-dry Riesling, Pinot Grigio/Pinot Gris, or Gewürztraminer for whites, and Gamay or Beaujolais for reds. If you're used to reaching for a beer to drink with Asian food, consider one of the inexpensive sparkling wines in this book.

FOOD MATCHES FOR SPARKLING WINE & CHAMPAGNE

- Dry (brut) sparkling wine and Champagne go well with appetizers of seafood, chicken, or cream cheese, and with dishes featuring seafood, veal, chicken, or turkey, particularly if served in a cream sauce.

- Some desserts, especially those with fruit, pair well with sweeter, fruitier sparkling wines. Make sure the wine is sweeter than the dessert, or the wine will seem sour.

WINE & CHEESE MATCHES

Wine and cheese are thought to go together like love and marriage but, quite often, the match is not made in heaven. Here are some that are.

- Parmigiano-Reggiano, Manchego, aged cheddar, and some other full-flavoured and harder cheeses go well with full-flavoured red wines such as Cabernet Sauvignon, Bordeaux, Rioja, and Amarone.
- Roquefort, Stilton, and other blue-veined cheeses tend to go better with sweet white wines, like icewine and late-harvest wine. Port and Stilton are a classic match.
- Goat cheese and Sauvignon Blanc go extremely well together.
- Brie, Camembert, and other soft, creamy, and mild-flavoured cheeses go well with Chardonnay and lighter Pinot Noir.
- Smoked cheeses pair well with slightly sweet sherry, off-dry Gewürz-traminer, or late-harvest wine.

ARGENTINA

ARGENTINA IS ONE OF THE WORLD's largest wine-producers (it ranks fifth), so it's surprising that the LCBO stocks such a small number of Argentinean wines. Although it's better known for red wine, Argentina turns out some excellent whites, too. Most are made from the varieties most popular in international markets like Ontario: Chardonnay, Pinot Grigio/Pinot Gris, and Sauvignon Blanc.

Argento Pinot Grigio 2007

★ ★ ★ ½

MENDOZA $10.10   (620492)

Wine has been made in Argentina (and in Mendoza) since the 1500s,
but the attention given to Pinot Grigio is much more recent. This is a nice
example that gets away from the common fruity style to one that's crisp
and refreshing and in many ways better with food. Look for well-defined
flavours and a dry and zesty texture, and serve it with slightly spicy seafood.

NOTES
....
....
....
....

Astica Sauvignon Blanc/Semillon 2007

★ ★ ★ ½

MENDOZA $8.10   (359083)

The blend of Sauvignon Blanc and Semillon has a long history, but it got
its modern push from Australia. This example from Argentina introduces
another style with a little more influence from the Sauvignon's zestiness.
The influence of the Semillon, adding some creaminess in the texture, is
still there and the combination is very appealing. Drink it with grilled
white fish and seafood.

NOTES
....
....
....
....

Funky Llama Chardonnay 2007

★ ★ ★

MENDOZA $10.10   (614677)

It was probably inevitable, given the popularity of furry animals on labels,
that an Argentinean or Chilean winery was going to use a llama, funky
or otherwise. The Chardonnay inside the bottle isn't funky, though. It's a
well-made, straightforward wine that performs nicely in flavour, texture,
and balance. There's nothing to rave about here, but nothing not to like.
Drink it with chicken, pork, or fish.

NOTES
....
....
....
....
....

★ ★ ★ ★

Lurton Pinot Gris 2007

MENDOZA $10.95   (556746)

The Lurton brothers make wine all over the world—and do so success-fully. This Pinot Gris from their Argentinean winery delivers very attrac-tive and intense aromas and flavours. It's plush, mouth filling, and quite stylish, with food-friendly edginess, and it makes a great wine for spicy seafood and Asian dishes.

NOTES

....

....

....

....

★ ★ ★

Marcus James Chardonnay 2007

MENDOZA $9.30   (372672)

This is wine with New World all over it. It's assertively fruit forward, with rich flavours, and they come at you with a dense texture. It might sound a bit too much—and there is a lot here—but it all works quite well, thanks largely to the good seam of acidity that pulls everything into shape and keeps the fruit on a leash. Drink this with something substantial, like grilled or roast pork.

NOTES

....

....

....

....

★ ★ ★ ½

Trapiche Chardonnay 2007

MENDOZA $8.80   (588004)

Trapiche makes many of the LCBO's Argentinean wines, and they show that large producers can turn out some very good wines. This is a nicely made Chardonnay, showing attractive fruit flavours with a hint of spici-ness. It's medium bodied and smooth textured, with a fresh edginess to suit food. It goes very well with the rotisserie chicken you pick up on your way home from work.

NOTES

....

....

....

....

AUSTRALIA

ALTHOUGH AUSTRALIA IS BETTER KNOWN FOR red wine, especially Shiraz, it produces a wide range of whites, too. The most common variety is Chardonnay but others, such as the Semillon/Sauvignon Blanc blend so popular in Australia, also cross the Pacific Ocean.

The most common regional designation for Australian wine is South Eastern Australia, a mega-zone that represents more than 90 percent of Australia's wine production and many of its wine regions. The well-known smaller wine regions include South Australia, Western Australia, and Victoria (which are all states).

Banrock Station Chardonnay 2007

★ ★ ★ ★

SOUTH EASTERN AUSTRALIA $9.95 (463943)

Banrock Station is heavily involved in environmental issues, and part of the revenue from sales in Ontario supports the "Bring Back the Salmon" campaign to reintroduce Atlantic salmon to Lake Ontario. This is an attractive Chardonnay, with well-defined and quite concentrated ripe, fruity flavours. It has a smooth texture with a refreshing edge that makes it food friendly. Drink it with pork chops or chicken. Not with salmon.

NOTES

....

....

....

....

Banrock Station Unwooded Chardonnay 2007

★ ★ ★ ½

SOUTH EASTERN AUSTRALIA $10.95 (455022)

[1-Litre Tetra Pak] The point of producing unwooded Chardonnay is to present the fruit flavours and texture without the influence of oak in any form (barrels, staves, or chips). In principle, it leads to more pure and vibrant versions of both. It does in this case. You'll find this is a zesty, medium-bodied Chardonnay that's refreshing as an aperitif or as a wine to drink with fish and seafood.

NOTES

....

....

....

....

Black Opal Chardonnay 2007

★ ★ ★

SOUTH EASTERN AUSTRALIA $14.00 (309450)

Opals are one of the popular souvenirs that tourists bring back from Australia. They're available in an infinite number of colours and patterns, but this little gem of a Chardonnay comes in black. This is all about the popular style of Australian Chardonnay—rich flavours, a fruit-forward style, a smooth and mouth-filling texture. It's well balanced and complements a range of dishes, including chicken and pork.

NOTES

....

....

....

....

Cookoothama Chardonnay 2006
★ ★ ★ ★ ½   RIVERINA $13.95   (619403)

This is a particularly opulent Chardonnay. The flavours come on in a series of rich layers and the texture is creamy, silky, and voluptuous. At the same time, there's enough acidity to cut through the richness and head off any potential sweetness. It really is an outstanding effort. This is almost a bit too intense for sipping so, instead, drink it with a full-flavoured dish featuring lobster or turkey.

NOTES

Hardys 'Nottage Hill' Chardonnay 2007
★ ★ ★ ½   SOUTH EASTERN AUSTRALIA $11.45   (283457)

Thomas Hardy, who founded this winery, was a hardy settler who was producing more than 600,000 bottles of wine a year by the 1880s. Who knows how that wine tasted, but it was probably nothing like this well-made, medium-bodied Chardonnay, with its attractive and concentrated flavours. It has a soft but quite refreshing texture, and goes well with pizza topped with smoked chicken.

NOTES

Hardys 'Stamp of Australia' Riesling/Gewürztraminer 2007
★ ★ ★ ½   SOUTH EASTERN AUSTRALIA $9.95   (448548)

This is an off-dry (meaning slightly sweet) blend that combines the strengths of the two grape varieties: the refreshing texture of Riesling and the rich, pungent flavours of Gewürztraminer. Overall, it's quite stylish, with bright and concentrated fruit, and a crisp texture. It's medium bodied and goes well with spicy Asian food, so try it next time you get Thai takeout.

NOTES

★ ★ ★ ½

Lindemans 'Bin 65' Chardonnay 2007

SOUTH EASTERN AUSTRALIA $11.95   (142117)

Bin 65 was designed specifically for the Canadian market because of the popularity of this style of wine here. Launched in 1985, it quickly became an icon throughout the world. Year after year, it delivers solid ripe fruit flavours, a clean, smooth, and slightly edgy texture, and good balance. It isn't too much of anything but has enough of everything to make it a versatile food wine. Drink it with roast pork or chicken.

NOTES

....

....

....

....

★ ★ ★ ½

Lindemans 'Bin 95' Sauvignon Blanc 2007

SOUTH EASTERN AUSTRALIA $11.40   (181388)

Australian wineries originally gave their wines bin numbers according to where the bottles were stored. Bin 95 is a light- to medium-bodied Sauvignon with a crisp, almost zesty texture, and good lively fruit flavours. It's clean and refreshing, very good for sipping on a hot day, or drinking with grilled fish or seafood with lemon juice.

NOTES

....

....

....

....

....

★ ★ ★ ½

Little Penguin Chardonnay 2007

SOUTH EASTERN AUSTRALIA $11.75   (598904)

This little bird has big flavours. It's a fruit-forward Chardonnay in the style that swept the world in the 1990s and that still has a massive amount of support. There are hints of oak along with the fruit, and the texture is plush, smooth, and mouth filling. It's medium bodied and well balanced, and is great with pork, well-seasoned chicken, or leftover-turkey sandwiches.

NOTES

....

....

....

....

....

MadFish Sauvignon Blanc/Semillon 2006

★ ★ ★ ★

WESTERN AUSTRALIA $15.15   (588863)

This is another winner from Western Australia, where they don't seem to be able to make any wine missteps. Quite what this fish is mad about isn't clear. Not the wine, which is a very attractive blend of refreshing Sauvignon zestiness and solid Semillon roundness. These two varieties form wonderful partnerships, and together they create a happy relationship with grilled fish.

NOTES

....

....

....

....

....

McWilliam's 'Hanwood Estate' Chardonnay 2006

★ ★ ★ ★

SOUTH EASTERN AUSTRALIA $13.50   (557934)

McWilliam's is a large winery that's still family run—rare today when multinational corporations own most big wineries. This Chardonnay gets marks for elegance. It delivers lovely, complex flavours with a subtle hint of oak from the aging. It's medium bodied with a smooth texture, and is a natural for chicken, fish, pork, or seafood in a cream sauce.

NOTES

....

....

....

....

Penfolds 'Koonunga Hill' Chardonnay 2006

★ ★ ★ ★

SOUTH EASTERN AUSTRALIA $15.45   (321943)

Dr. Christopher Penfold started making wine in Australia in the 1840s and prescribed it to his settler patients for the anemia many had after their long voyage from Britain. Now we drink it for pleasure, and you can certainly enjoy the intense, ripe fruit flavours in this Chardonnay. It's medium bodied and very well balanced, and has a rich, attractive texture. Drink it with roast pork or turkey.

NOTES

....

....

....

....

Rosemount 'Diamond Label' Chardonnay 2006

★ ★ ★

SOUTH EASTERN AUSTRALIA $16.00 (265132)

The original Rosemount winery really is on a rise in the topography, and is liberally planted with roses. It has established a reputation for wines of quality and value, and this Chardonnay certainly delivers. The flavours are concentrated and ripe, and it's mouth filling and smooth with a nice line of acidity that makes it friendly to food. Drink this with roast chicken or grilled pork chops.

NOTES
....
....
....
....

Rosemount 'Diamond Label' Sauvignon Blanc 2007

★ ★ ★ ½

SOUTH EASTERN AUSTRALIA $16.00 (329573)

Don't worry that the wine looks green in the bottle. It's the bottle. In your glass it's a very pale yellow, but don't let the paleness fool you into thinking this will be a wine with little flavour. There's plenty of bright fruit here, and it's complemented by the zesty, vibrant texture. This wine makes your mouth sing. To make even more music, eat some freshly shucked oysters. Then sip the wine. Repeat until finished.

NOTES
....
....
....
....

Rosemount 'Diamond Label' Traminer/Riesling 2007

★ ★ ★ ½

SOUTH EASTERN AUSTRALIA $12.45 (244301)

There is a grape variety called Traminer, but in many parts of the world (including Australia) the name is also used to refer to Gewürztraminer— maybe because it's easier to pronounce. With its sweet pungency and Riesling's zesty crispness, the blend is pretty compelling, especially if you're looking for a wine to have with spicy Thai food. It's semi-sweet, with a good lively texture that tones down the sweetness nicely.

NOTES
....
....
....
....

Wolf Blass 'Bilyara Reserve' Chardonnay 2006

★ ★ ★ ★ ½

SOUTH AUSTRALIA $13.85   (8128)

[PET Bottle] This is bottled in PET, a food-grade plastic that's much lighter than glass. It looks as if you're getting less, but this is a regular-volume bottle. And the wine is quite big. It's characterized by full and luscious fruit flavours, with a lot of complexity, while the texture is mouth filling and smooth. Still, it's refreshing, and makes an excellent choice for roast turkey or cold lobster.

NOTES

....

....

....

....

Wolf Blass 'Red Label' Semillon/Sauvignon Blanc 2007

★ ★ ★ ½

SOUTH EASTERN AUSTRALIA $14.45   (323063)

A popular blend in Australia (where it's called "Sem-Sauv"), this combines varieties often found in white Bordeaux wines. Wolf Blass's medium-bodied example has a rich, mouth-filling texture (from the Semillon) combined with light and refreshing crispness (from the Sauvignon Blanc). It has focused and refreshing flavours, and goes very well with fish and chips sprinkled with lemon juice.

NOTES

....

....

....

....

Wolf Blass 'Yellow Label' Chardonnay 2007

★ ★ ★ ★

SOUTH AUSTRALIA $16.00   (226860)

Wolf Blass "Yellow Label" Cabernet Sauvignon was Wolfie's first big hit in Ontario, and now the LCBO's shelves have more of his mellow yellow labels. This is a big Chardonnay, fruit forward and the sort of wine that should have wide appeal. What gives it quality and value is the complexity of the flavours and the refreshing texture, which makes this a great choice for fish, chicken, or pork dishes.

NOTES

....

....

....

....

Wolf Blass 'Yellow Label' Riesling 2007

★ ★ ★ ★

SOUTH AUSTRALIA $14.85   (505370)

Australia has been a leader in combining Riesling and screw cap closures. They seem to be a perfect match, with the screw caps protecting the fresh fruitiness of the young wine. Taste it here, in a Riesling that has lively and vibrant flavours with good complexity, and a texture to match. It's both substantial and refreshing, and is an excellent choice for grilled or sautéed seafood.

NOTES

....

....

....

....

Yellow Tail Semillon/Sauvignon Blanc 2008

★ ★ ★

SOUTH EASTERN AUSTRALIA $11.20   (640136)

Yellow Tail Shiraz swept North American (and other) markets in the early 2000s, and other varieties were gradually added to the list. This Sem-Sauv (a blend that's very popular in Australia) delivers solid fruit flavour without a lot of complexity, and a refreshing and crisp texture. It's ideal for sipping during the summer and also goes well with grilled seafood and simply prepared white fish.

NOTES

....

....

....

....

BRITISH COLUMBIA

BRITISH COLUMBIA'S WINERIES PRODUCE QUALITY and value-priced white wine, but you won't find very many on LCBO shelves. Don't blame the LCBO. The reason is that British Columbians love their wine and drink most of what's made in their province.

The Vintners Quality Alliance (VQA) classification on British Columbia wine labels means that the grapes were grown in the region specified and that the wine has been tested and tasted to ensure quality.

Mission Hill Reserve Chardonnay 2005

★ ★ ★ ★ ½

VQA OKANAGAN VALLEY $22.00   (545004)

[Vintages Essential] Mission Hill is the Okanagan Valley's icon winery, a tourist destination that attracts crowds to see its architecture and site, and to taste its well-made wines. This Chardonnay is rich and elegant, with intense, upfront fruit flavours, and a smooth, mouth-filling texture. It's nicely balanced, with the crispness needed to make it work well with food. Try it with grilled salmon.

NOTES

....

....

....

....

....

Wild Horse Canyon Chardonnay 2006

★ ★ ★ ½

BRITISH COLUMBIA/WASHINGTON/CALIFORNIA

$12.95   (54437)

This is a blend of wines from three regions, but British Columbia is first on the list, which suggests it might have contributed more than either of the other two. Inter-regional blending is common enough elsewhere, so why not in North America? You get a well-made Chardonnay with solid, round flavours and good balance. It's refreshing and tangy, and makes a good partner for chicken, pork, and seafood dishes.

NOTES

....

....

....

....

....

....

CALIFORNIA

CALIFORNIA GROWS A WIDE RANGE OF white grapes, but it's best known for Chardonnay, which is its most popular and widely planted variety. Still, don't overlook other quality whites, especially Pinot Grigio and Sauvignon Blanc. Napa Valley is the state's most famous region, but most of the value wines in this book are designated simply "California." This means that producers can source grapes from any region in the state.

Barefoot Pinot Grigio

★ ★ ★

CALIFORNIA $9.95   (53983)

[Non-vintage] A non-vintage wine means that it's a blend of two or more
vintages, none of them in a big enough proportion to allow the wine to
be labelled with a vintage year. (Many vintage-dated wines can contain
a small percentage of wine from other years.) This is simply well made, a
straightforward Pinot Grigio without pretension. The flavours are solid,
it's well balanced and has the fruitiness to handle a fairly spicy Thai dish.

NOTES

....

....

....

....

Beaulieu Vineyard 'BV Coastal Estates' Sauvignon Blanc 2006

★ ★ ★ ★

CALIFORNIA $13.05   (295253)

It might seem odd to get a cool-climate wine like Sauvignon Blanc from
sunny California, but sunny doesn't always mean hot. There are plenty
of cooler regions where these grapes ripen and retain their acidity, as this
bottle shows. The flavours are rich and complex, the texture has all the
zestiness you look for in a Sauvignon Blanc, and the finish is concentrated
and full. Food? Try grilled white fish with fresh lemon juice.

NOTES

....

....

....

....

Beringer 'Founders' Estate' Pinot Grigio 2006

★ ★ ★ ★ ½

CALIFORNIA $17.95   (45641)

This is a delicious Pinot Grigio that delivers real stylishness and elegance.
The flavours are well defined with both concentration and delicacy, and
the texture shows a beautiful balance of acidity and fruit. It's silky smooth
and has a refreshing quality that suits it to food, although you could
savour it on its own, too. If you're thinking of food, serve it with a deli-
cately spiced Thai dish.

NOTES

....

....

....

Beringer 'Stone Cellars' Chardonnay 2006

★ ★ ★ ½

CALIFORNIA $14.00   (606806)

"Stone Cellars" refers to the cellars carved into the cliff face at the Beringer winery in the late 19th century. They provided the coolness and humidity needed for wine aging in barrels. This is a Chardonnay made in a popular style. It has quite rich, luscious, and fruity flavours and a texture that's mouth filling, smooth, and well balanced. Dry and medium-weight, it's a good wine for roast or grilled chicken or pork.

NOTES

....

....

....

....

Bonterra Vineyards Chardonnay 2006

★ ★ ★ ★ ½

MENDOCINO COUNTY $18.95   (342436)

[Vintages Essential] Bonterra farms its vineyards organically, which is to say without chemical and artificial fertilizers, herbicides, or pesticides. Some people are suspicious of organic wines, but they should taste this excellent Chardonnay. It has flavours that are concentrated and complex, and a full but lively and refreshing texture. The balance is just excellent, and this goes beautifully with freshwater fish and roast chicken.

NOTES

....

....

....

....

Conundrum 2006

★ ★ ★ ★

CALIFORNIA $26.95   (694653)

[Vintages Essential] The conundrum, or puzzle, here is which grape varieties are used to make this wine. Giving away the answer won't ruin your enjoyment of the wine (we're not talking movie plots here), so it's safe to say that it's a blend of Chardonnay, Sauvignon Blanc, Viognier, and Muscat Canelli. They add up to a gorgeous off-dry wine with delicious layered, complex flavours and a plush, refreshing texture that's perfect with spicy Asian dishes.

NOTES

....

....

....

....

Fetzer 'Valley Oaks' Chardonnay 2007

★★★★

CALIFORNIA $14.00   (291674)

This is a Chardonnay that's quietly stylish right through. The aromas and flavours are fairly concentrated, but they're not what one winemaker calls "stand on a rake" flavours—the ones that smack you in the face. The texture is smooth and full, with a refreshing quality. All in all, a successful Chardonnay you can sip without food or enjoy with lighter chicken and seafood dishes.

NOTES

....

....

....

....

Fetzer 'Valley Oaks' Fumé Blanc 2006

★★★ ½

CALIFORNIA $14.00   (255448)

Fetzer cultivates its vineyards sustainably, without using chemical fertilizers and pesticides. In this Fumé Blanc (which is Sauvignon Blanc—and called "Blanc Fumé" in some parts of France's Loire Valley) you'll find attractive, reasonably complex fruit, and a surprisingly full and generous texture that's clean and refreshing. Medium-bodied and dry, it's well made and is a fine complement to pork tenderloin or chicken.

NOTES

....

....

....

....

Fish Eye Pinot Grigio 2007

★★★ ½

CALIFORNIA $10.00   (614263)

If you're looking for a wine to go with spicy dishes, like pad Thai or garlic shrimp, this might be the one. It isn't sweet, but it's really fruity, with luscious, ripe flavours that go very well with spicy dishes. It's medium bodied, smooth textured, even a little creamy, and it has a refreshing quality that makes it ideal for food.

NOTES

....

....

....

....

Francis Ford Coppola Presents Pinot Grigio 2006
★ ★ ★

CALIFORNIA $14.95   (56424)

This is a Pinot Grigio on the heavier and fatter side. The flavours are nicely concentrated and full of ripe fruit, and the texture is more mouth filling, round, and creamy than you usually find in a Pinot Grigio. It tastes and feels attractive, although it might be a bit difficult to match with food. This is best drunk as an aperitif or with varied light appetizers.

NOTES

....

....

....

....

....

Gnarly Head Chardonnay 2006
★ ★ ★ ★

CALIFORNIA $16.95   (68932)

There's a lot of character in this Chardonnay, starting with the zesty, clean, and mouth-filling texture you feel at your first sip. It rolls out flavours that are concentrated, layered, and complex, and which harmonize very nicely with the texture. It's dry and medium bodied and is versatile with food. Try it with chicken, pork, or turkey, or even with seared scallops.

NOTES

....

....

....

....

....

Gray Fox Chardonnay 2007
★ ★ ★ ½

CALIFORNIA $7.90   (614271)

Another critter, another Chardonnay . . . but wait, this isn't bad at all! In fact it's pretty good. There's a lot of fruit in this wine, and the texture is mouth filling, smooth, and balanced so that it's refreshing. Overall, it's well made and a real bargain at the price. This is a good choice for a wide range of food: chicken, pork, fish, or seafood.

NOTES

....

....

....

....

R.H. Phillips 'Toasted Head' Chardonnay 2006

★ ★ ★ ★
CALIFORNIA $17.95   (594341)

[Vintages Essential] "Toasted head" refers to the practice of charring the insides of barrels before they're used for aging wine. Often the ends (the heads) are not toasted, but in the barrels used to age this Chardonnay, they were. This is a bold and assertive wine with concentrated flavours and a mouth-filling texture, but with the lightness needed for it to pair well with food. Drink it with grilled salmon or pork tenderloin.

NOTES
....
....
....
....

Robert Mondavi Fumé Blanc 2006

★ ★ ★ ★
NAPA VALLEY $24.95   (221887)

[Vintages Essential] It's said Robert Mondavi coined the name "Fumé Blanc" because of the smoky flavours he detected in some Sauvignon Blancs. You might discern a touch of smokiness in this one, which possesses quite pungent and intense flavours. With its more-than-medium body and smooth and refreshing texture, this Fumé Blanc goes well with freshly shucked oysters or with grilled white fish and a squeeze of lemon.

NOTES
....
....
....
....

Robert Mondavi 'Private Selection' Chardonnay 2006

★ ★ ★ ★ ½
CENTRAL COAST $17.95   (379180)

[Vintages Essential] Try this on any Chardonnay skeptic—you know, the people who loudly declare that they don't like Chardonnay, as if it's something to be proud of. Chardonnay comes in so many styles, and this is a particularly attractive one. It's medium to full bodied, has a smooth texture, and lovely concentrated flavours. It's a versatile, fruit-filled Chardonnay that goes as well with roast chicken as with grilled salmon.

NOTES
....
....
....
....

Smoking Loon Chardonnay 2005

★ ★ ★ ½

CALIFORNIA $17.95   (55509)

This is not a wine for anti-tobacco activists. The plastic cork is printed with "Whooh Whooh Whooh *Cough* Whooh Whooh *Cough*." Whooh knows whooh came up with the name, or what it signifies. Does it matter? This is a nicely made, barrel-aged California Chardonnay that delivers good solid flavours and an attractively tangy texture. It's a good choice for chicken or pork.

NOTES
....
....
....
....

Sonoma Vineyards Chardonnay 2005

★ ★ ★ ★

SONOMA COUNTY $19.45   (60624)

Sonoma Vineyards is a brand of Rodney Strong, which has a solid reputation for making fine wines. This Chardonnay delivers in every respect. The flavours are dominated by ripe fruit, with a core of sweetness and radiating layers of complexity. It's smooth and fresh in texture, medium in weight, and an ideal wine for roast turkey with cranberries, or pork and applesauce.

NOTES
....
....
....
....

Sterling 'Vintner's Collection' Chardonnay 2006

★ ★ ★ ★ ½

CENTRAL COAST $16.05   (669242)

This is one luscious Chardonnay. It begins with aromas that are all ripe, sweet fruit and a hint of oak, and that quickly follow through (quickly, because as lovely as the aromas are, you wonder how it tastes) to beautifully complex and nuanced flavours. The texture is mouth filling with an attractive edginess. All in all, a fine wine at a very good price. Drink it with chicken, turkey, grilled salmon, or pork.

NOTES
....
....
....
....

Turning Leaf Reserve Chardonnay 2005

★ ★ ★ ½

CALIFORNIA $12.35   (409805)

Turning Leaf has been a standby for many consumers over the years, and it delivers consistent quality for the price. This Chardonnay has an easy-drinking style that makes it a great choice for large gatherings. The flavours are well defined without being intense, and the texture is soft and smooth and nicely balanced. It works as a wine to sip on its own or to drink with roast chicken or pork tenderloin.

NOTES

....

....

....

....

Twin Fin Chardonnay 2005

★ ★ ★

CALIFORNIA $12.95   (38315)

This is a perfect Chardonnay for the consumer depicted on the label: hip, surfing, convertible-driving, with all his hair . . . but why is he alone? The Chardonnay is a crowd-pleaser, so he must be meeting all his friends at the beach. After they've surfed their hearts out (remembering not to drink and surf!), they'll enjoy its fruity flavours and full, smooth texture, maybe with chicken that they'll cook over a bonfire on the sand.

NOTES

....

....

....

....

Twin Fin Pinot Grigio 2006

★ ★ ★ ½

CALIFORNIA $12.95   (38323)

If you're looking for a change from Italian Pinot Grigio, test drive this one. The label expresses the laid-back image of California, and this is a popular white to take to the beach, the patio, or the cottage. It's fresh and crisp, with good fruit flavours. Not too complex but just very well made, it's perfect for sipping on its own and pairs successfully with spicy fish, seafood, and chicken.

NOTES

....

....

....

....

Virgin Vines Chardonnay 2006

★ ★ ★ ½

CALIFORNIA $14.00   (18598)

This sits on the bolder and fruitier end of the spectrum of Chardonnay styles. It's medium-plus in body, with a generous, mouth-filling texture, and it tends towards what's called "fat" in wine-speak—meaning that it's relatively low in acidity. With full fruit flavours, this works well with rich white meats, such as roast pork with slightly tart applesauce to balance the wine's fruitiness.

NOTES

....

....

....

....

Wente 'Morning Fog' Chardonnay 2006

★ ★ ★ ★ ½

LIVERMORE VALLEY/SAN FRANCISCO BAY $16.05   (175430)

The morning fog is important to many California wine regions. It swirls up the river valleys early in the day and keeps the vines cool until it eventually dissipates late morning or early afternoon. The results are in Chardonnays like this, that retain wonderful freshness of taste and texture while having concentrated flavours and a round, silky mouth feel. It's a delicious wine with chicken, turkey, or pork.

NOTES

....

....

....

....

Woodbridge Sauvignon Blanc 2007

★ ★ ★ ½

CALIFORNIA $10.95   (40501)

Compare this to the Robert Mondavi Fumé Blanc: Same producer and grape variety, but different brand, different varietal name, and a very different price. Why not buy both and taste-test them? This one is really very vibrant and zesty, with nicely pitched flavours that are bright, fresh and pure. No question that this is destined for shellfish, seafood, or fish that's been subjected to a squeeze of fresh lemon.

NOTES

....

....

....

....

CHILE

ALTHOUGH CHILE IS BETTER KNOWN for its red wines, many of its whites offer great quality and value. The warm growing conditions in most of Chile's wine regions have led many producers to seek out cooler areas and to plant vines at higher (and cooler) altitudes. The main whites are Chardonnay and Sauvignon Blanc, but there are others.

Designated wine regions are indicated after the letters "DO" (*Denominación de Origen*).

Caliterra Reserva Sauvignon Blanc 2007

★ ★ ★

DO CURICÓ VALLEY $10.95   (275909)

The regions generally considered best for Sauvignon Blanc are the Loire Valley in France and Marlborough in New Zealand, but Chile produces well-priced competition. This one from Caliterra has a crisp, refreshing texture and vibrant, fresh fruit flavours. It's light- to medium-bodied and goes well with a goat cheese salad or with seafood juiced with a fresh lemon.

NOTES

....

....

....

....

....

Carmen Chardonnay 2006

★ ★ ★ ½

DO CASABLANCA VALLEY $9.90   (235663)

The Casablanca Valley is cooled in early afternoon by winds that blow in from the nearby Pacific Ocean. You can feel the freshness on your face as you stand in the valley. It cools the grapes, too, and they pick up the acidity that gives this Chardonnay its refreshing texture. Add attractive fruit flavours, and you have a wine you can sip as an aperitif or drink with seafood or shellfish, not to mention chicken.

NOTES

....

....

....

....

....

Casillero del Diablo Chardonnay 2006

★ ★ ★ ½

DO CENTRAL VALLEY $10.95   (58420)

Concha y Toro's Casillero del Diablo line is successful across the board, whether you're playing the red or the white. This is a very attractive Chardonnay that should please anyone, and pairs well with chicken, pork, or fish. It's got fairly rich flavours and a quite plush and weighty feel. At the same time, there's a nice seam of acidity that leaves your palate feeling refreshed.

NOTES

....

....

....

....

Cousiño-Macul 'Doña Isidora' Riesling 2007
★ ★ ★ ★ ★
DO MAIPO VALLEY $11.95   (57182)

This is a luscious Riesling—a variety that's not all that common in
Chile—from one of the country's premium producers. Everything is in
place here, from the quite elegant aromas with the telltale whiff of petrol,
the concentrated and nuanced flavours, and the medium-weight, balanced, and crisp texture. This is a dry Riesling and an excellent wine to
serve with grilled shrimp.

NOTES

Errazuriz Chardonnay 2007
★ ★ ★ ★ ½
DO CASABLANCA VALLEY $11.80   (318741)

This is a lovely Chardonnay, the sort to serve to those who say they don't
like the variety. Just make sure they don't know what it is. They'll be
hard pressed to resist its luscious fruit flavours, medium-to-full body, and
smooth texture with the crispness needed to go with food. When you're
pouring this for friends, go all out and serve some rotisserie chicken, too.

NOTES

Espiritu de Chile Sauvignon Blanc 2006
★ ★ ★ ½
DO CENTRAL VALLEY $10.95   (60640)

Chile's Central Valley lies north-south between the Andes and a coastal
range. Rivers fed by the melting snow in the Andes irrigate the vineyards.
This quite stylish Sauvignon Blanc does a good job of delivering the
variety's classic flavours (concentrated and pungent) and texture (full and
zesty). It's a natural for grilled white fish with fresh lemon juice.

NOTES

Santa Alicia Reserve Chardonnay 2006

★ ★ ★ ★

DO MAIPO VALLEY $11.00   (414474)

The grapes for this wine were grown in one of Chile's larger wine regions, but at a higher elevation. There they find conditions that are cooler than the areas on the valley floor, yet warm enough for the grapes to ripen fully. The result is this wine with concentrated and quite rich flavours, and a texture that's both full and refreshing. It's dry and medium bodied, and it goes well with roast chicken or a supermarket barbecued chicken.

NOTES

....

....

....

....

Santa Carolina Reserva Chardonnay 2007

★ ★ ★ ½

DO CASABLANCA VALLEY $11.85   (304022)

Sometimes the world seems to be awash in Chardonnay, but remember that it comes in many styles, from lean and crisp to fat and buttery in your mouth. This is in the mid-range. It's mouth filling and plush, with rich, pungent flavours. At the same time, it has some crispness that ensures it goes well with many kinds of food. Try it with roast chicken or grilled pork chops.

NOTES

....

....

....

....

Santa Carolina Reserva Sauvignon Blanc 2007

★ ★ ★ ½

DO RAPEL VALLEY $11.85   (337535)

The grapes for this wine were grown in the foothills of the Andes, that magnificent snow-topped range that you can see from almost anywhere in Chile. The crisp early mornings are reflected in the brisk freshness of this wine, while the flavours are nicely concentrated and focused. Dry and medium bodied, this goes very well with grilled white fish and seafood, or with mussels steamed in white wine.

NOTES

....

....

....

....

THE 500 BEST-VALUE WINES IN THE LCBO | 2009

CHILE | THE WHITES

Santa Carolina Sauvignon Blanc 2007
★★★ ½   DO RAPEL VALLEY $9.75   (269579)

This is an attractive Sauvignon Blanc with a zesty and refreshing texture. It's not tart or sour, but it's the sort that wakes up your palate and makes you feel like eating. In this case you might try grilled white fish or shrimp with fresh lemon juice, or a warm goat cheese salad. Food like that will play off the texture and the quite concentrated and pungent flavours.

NOTES

Santa Rita '120' Sauvignon Blanc 2007
★★★ ½   DO LONTUÉ VALLEY $10.45   (23606)

Sauvignon Blanc has been "discovered" in the last ten years and this has led to plantings in many different conditions. In turn, many different styles have emerged, and this example from Santa Rita sits in the middle. It has quite full flavours but retains the crisp tanginess of texture that makes Sauvignon Blanc such a good wine to go with white fish and seafood.

NOTES

Santa Rita Reserva Chardonnay 2006
★★★★   DO CASABLANCA VALLEY $13.95   (348359)

Santa Rita is one of Chile's established wineries, but it doesn't rest on its well-deserved laurels. The evidence is in this Casablanca Chardonnay, grown in a relatively recently developed, cool region that produces fresh, crisp, and well-focused wines. The flavours are concentrated, the texture tangy and refreshing, and the overall image attractive. Serve it with grilled pork tenderloin.

NOTES

48

Santa Rita Reserva Sauvignon Blanc 2007

★ ★ ★ ★

DO CASABLANCA VALLEY $13.50   (275677)

Sauvignon Blanc is popular because of its characteristic crisp texture and clean, pungent flavours, which it develops when the grapes grow in cooler areas. The vineyards in Chile's Casablanca Valley are cooled by breezes that blow in from the Pacific Ocean early each afternoon. You can taste them in the zesty texture and lovely flavours of this Sauvignon Blanc, which is great served with fish or seafood spritzed with lemon.

NOTES

....

....

....

....

Tarapaca Sauvignon Blanc 2007

★ ★ ★ ★

DO MAIPO VALLEY $9.90   (414185)

The time-honoured food matches for Sauvignon Blanc include fresh oysters and goat cheese. Both are rich and salty, and go well with the fruit and zestiness of many Sauvignon Blancs. This one from Tarapaca (the stress is on the last *a*) has dense and pungent flavours. It's medium bodied and quite zesty, and goes well with either of the classic food pairings.

NOTES

....

....

....

....

....

Trio Sauvignon Blanc 2007

★ ★ ★ ★

DO CASABLANCA VALLEY $12.85   (678656)

While other wines from Concha y Toro's "Trio" range are blends of three grape varieties, the name here refers to a trio of vineyards in the cool Casablanca Valley. This region is getting a deserved reputation for producing very good Sauvignon Blanc, and here it delivers concentrated flavours, a zesty texture, and excellent balance. It complements a wide range of seafood but goes especially well with oysters.

NOTES

....

....

....

....

FRANCE

FRANCE PRODUCES WHITE WINES from many different grape varieties. Some regions are closely tied to specific grapes, like Burgundy to Chardonnay, but others are not. You'll find a wide range of varieties and styles in this list.

French wine labels show a few terms worth knowing. Wines labelled *Appellation d'Origine Contrôlée* (AOC in this book) are wines in France's highest quality classification. They're made under tight rules that regulate aspects like the grape varieties that can be used in each region.

Wines labelled *Vin de Pays* are regional wines made with fewer restrictions. They must be good quality, but producers have much more flexibility in the grapes they can use and how much wine they can make. *Vin de Pays d'Oc* (the ancient region of Occitanie) is by far the most important of the Vins de Pays wines.

Baron Philippe de Rothschild Chardonnay 2006

★ ★ ★ ½

VIN DE PAYS D'OC $10.95   (407528)

This producer has a prominent profile on the French wine scene, and this is its excursion into one of the hot (in more ways than one) regions of southern France. The result is a Chardonnay that's simply well made. It has concentrated and somewhat complex flavours and a fairly generous and refreshing texture. There's just nothing not to like here. Drink it with roast chicken, pork, turkey, grilled salmon, or seafood. It's that versatile.

NOTES

....

....

....

....

Bouchard Père & Fils Mâcon-Lugny Saint-Pierre 2006

★ ★ ★ ★

AOC MÂCON-LUGNY $15.25   (51573)

This is from a designated village in the Mâcon region in southern Burgundy. Made from 100 percent Chardonnay, this is an elegant wine that delivers nicely concentrated flavours that are soft and stylish. The texture is quite rich and creamy, with a seam of acidity that adds a refreshing note. It's an excellent wine for grilled salmon and for dishes featuring chicken, turkey, and pork.

NOTES

....

....

....

....

Bouchard Père & Fils Pouilly-Fuissé 2006

★ ★ ★ ★ ½

AOC POUILLY-FUISSÉ $27.90   (56580)

Pouilly-Fuissé is a famous region in southern Burgundy that produces only white wine and grows only Chardonnay. Don't expect to see this labelled as a Chardonnay, though, as the regional name is a selling point, as it should be for this one. It's gorgeous and stylish, with pure and nuanced flavours and a beautifully smooth and clean texture. Medium-weight and dry, it's a great choice for poultry, pork, fish, or seafood.

NOTES

....

....

....

....

★ ★ ★ ★ ½   **La Chablisienne 'Vieilles Vignes' Chablis 2005**

AOC CHABLIS $24.95   (942243)

[Vintages Essential] There's no standard definition of "old vines" (*vieilles vignes*) but producers often signal a wine made from them because older vines produce small quantities of higher quality grapes. This is certainly an elegant Chablis (made from Chardonnay), with stylish and nuanced flavours and a smooth, refreshing texture. Everything is in harmony and balance. Serve this with simply prepared fish, chicken, or pork dishes.

NOTES

....

....

....

....

★ ★ ★ ★ ½   **Château Bonnet Entre-Deux-Mers 2006**

AOC ENTRE-DEUX-MERS $13.05   (83709)

Entre-Deux-Mers, a Bordeaux wine region, means "between two seas"—a bit of an exaggeration because it's on a tongue of land between two rivers. But this wine isn't exaggerated. A blend of Sauvignon Blanc and Semillon, it has delicious concentrated flavours, all wrapped in a vibrant, crisp, and substantial texture. It's medium bodied and makes an excellent partner for grilled seafood and fish.

NOTES

....

....

....

....

★ ★ ★ ★   **Château de Sancerre 2006**

AOC SANCERRE $24.70   (340893)

The Sancerre wine region is at the eastern end of the Loire Valley, not far from Paris. The main grape variety is Sauvignon Blanc, and this example gives you classic Sauv Blanc character. Look for vibrant and pungent flavours, with a lively, refreshing texture that's also substantial. This wine has the heft to handle heavier food, such as pork or veal in a cream sauce.

NOTES

....

....

....

....

Dopff & Irion Gewürztraminer 2006
★ ★ ★ ★ ½
AOC ALSACE $16.45   (81463)

Gewürztraminer can be not only quite challenging to say and spell (thank God for self-service wine shopping), but it can be challenging as a wine, too. Take this lovely example. It's full of luscious fruit flavour and complexity, and has a plump and tangy texture. It's also off-dry—a little sweet. The answer is to sip it alone or drink it with spicy food, like Thai cuisine. Try it with a red or green curry.

NOTES

....

....

....

....

Fat Bastard Chardonnay 2007
★ ★ ★ ½
VIN DE PAYS D'OC $14.85   (563130)

Can you get tired of Chardonnay? Well, yes, if that's the only wine you drink. But if you intersperse your Chardonnays with other varieties, you'll better appreciate the range of this popular white. Here's one that's well balanced and offers lively but substantial flavours, and a generous, round, and refreshing texture. It's dry and medium bodied and is versatile with food. Try it with pork tenderloin or herbed roast chicken.

NOTES

....

....

....

....

Fortant Chardonnay 2006
★ ★ ★ ★
VIN DE PAYS D'OC $11.85   (433185)

Chardonnay is produced everywhere and in such huge volumes that it's an achievement to stand out from the crowd at any price point. This one, from the Skalli company, is a couple of notches above many others. It delivers quite lovely flavours with some complexity and a fairly generous and round texture that's also crisp and refreshing. It's a great choice for grilled salmon or chicken.

NOTES

....

....

....

....

Henri Bourgeois 'Les Baronnes' Sancerre 2006

★ ★ ★ ★ ½

AOC SANCERRE $24.95 (542548)

The grape variety used to make white Sancerre wine is Sauvignon Blanc, and Henri Bourgeois has had long experience with it. The producer even owns an estate in Marlborough, New Zealand's iconic Sauvignon region. "Les Baronnes" is a beautiful white, with vibrant and finely nuanced flavours and a texture that's smooth, mouth filling, and refreshing. This is a natural for grilled fish and seafood with a little fresh lemon juice.

NOTES

....
....
....
....

Louis Jadot Bourgogne Chardonnay 2007

★ ★ ★ ★

AOC BOURGOGNE $20.95 (933077)

[Vintages Essential] More and more French producers are adding the grape variety to the region on their labels (Chardonnay here, as well as Burgundy) to help consumers in our part of the world who buy by variety and not region. It makes no difference to the wine. In this case, it has a very attractive and complex flavour profile, and a smooth yet crisp texture. It's medium bodied and dry, and goes well with grilled fish and seafood.

NOTES

....
....
....
....

Louis Latour 'Ardèche' Chardonnay 2006

★ ★ ★ ★ ½

VIN DE PAYS DES COTEAUX DE L'ARDÈCHE $11.55 (132498)

This is an amazingly stylish Chardonnay from southwestern France. It's a couple of steps up from other Chardonnays at this price. Open it and you'll find the flavours are solid and intense but subtle, with layered complexity. The texture is deceptively soft at first, then comes through with a seam of refreshing acidity. Dry and medium-bodied, it's a fine choice for grilled fish, chicken, or pork.

NOTES

....
....
....
....

Lulu B. Chardonnay 2006

★★★ ½

VIN DE PAYS D'OC $11.95   (668996)

The Pays d'Oc wine region stretches over a broad expanse of France's Mediterranean zone. It produces a wide range of wines and some of the best values around. Lulu B. Chardonnay offers you good, upfront, and lively fruit flavours with a smooth, creamy, mouth-filling texture that has a subtle crispness making it good for food. You can drink this with pork, chicken, and turkey.

NOTES

....

....

....

....

Pierre Sparr Gewürztraminer 2006

★★★★

AOC ALSACE $16.05   (373373)

Pierre Sparr is an Alsatian producer who does well across his portfolio. This is a lovely medium-bodied Gewürztraminer with an opulent and plump texture that fills your mouth with spicy, pungent, and rich flavours that have complexity to spare. If you're looking for a sparring partner for this wine, try a spicy Asian (especially Thai) dish.

NOTES

....

....

....

....

....

Remy Pannier Anjou 2007

★★★ ½

AOC ANJOU $10.95   (5967)

Anjou is a wine region in the Loire Valley, and white wines there can be made from Chenin Blanc, Chardonnay, and Sauvignon Blanc. This seems to have a contribution from each. It has the ripe fruit flavours of Chenin Blanc, the body of Chardonnay, and the refreshing texture of Sauvignon Blanc. Overall, it's a lovely wine that's fruity, substantial, and clean. Sip it alone or drink it with chicken or seafood.

NOTES

....

....

....

....

Remy Pannier Muscadet Sèvre et Maine 2006

★ ★ ★ ½

AOC MUSCADET SÈVRE-ET-MAINE $10.95   (13821)

Muscadet is the fish wine of France—you'll find Muscadets on the wine list of every restaurant serving fish and seafood. Made from the Melon de Bourgogne grape, it's produced in the Loire Valley, near the Atlantic, and so it enhances the local cuisine. This Muscadet is light to medium in body, it's dry, and it has attractive crisp flavours and texture. It's just the thing for white fish and grilled seafood.

NOTES

Sauvion 'Carte d'Or' Muscadet 2006

★ ★ ★ ½

AOC MUSCADET SÈVRE-ET-MAINE $11.60   (143016)

Muscadet, from a Loire Valley region near the Atlantic coast, is France's most popular wine for fish and seafood. It can be bland and light, but this Muscadet has well-defined fruit flavours. It's medium bodied with an appealing and tangy texture, and it goes very well with seafood and fish. Try it with grilled white fish, or with mussels steamed in white wine.

NOTES

William Fèvre 'Champs Royaux' Chablis 2006

★ ★ ★ ★

AOC CHABLIS $22.50   (276436)

The classic wines from Chablis are Chardonnays made and aged in stainless steel tanks, not in oak barrels. They offer pure, bright fruit flavours like this one. It has a refreshing texture—not plush and mouth filling, but crisp and clean. It's medium bodied and makes an excellent match for shellfish. Try it with mussels steamed in white wine and garlic.

NOTES

Willm Réserve Riesling 2007

★ ★ ★ ★

AOC ALSACE $16.95   (11452)

Alsatian Riesling has a reputation all its own, and it's often the benchmark that New World Rieslings are judged against. This one from Willm
is quite luscious, with elegant flavours and the juicy, mouth-watering texture you expect from Riesling. It's dry, fruity, and medium bodied, and is
a great choice if you're eating shellfish or seafood—or you can sip it alone.

NOTES

....

....

....

....

....

....

Yvon Mau Colombard/Chardonnay 2007

★ ★ ★ ★

VIN DE PAYS DES CÔTES DE GASCOIGNE $9.25   (627265)

Colombard is a little-known grape variety from the west of France, now
often used for distilling into Cognac. But some is grown for wine, and
in this blend it delivers delicious fresh fruit flavours. It's almost medium
bodied with a clean, fruity, and refreshing texture. This is a great wine to
drink with chicken, fish, or seafood, especially when they're served in a
cream sauce.

NOTES

....

....

....

GERMANY

WONDERFUL, GOOD-VALUE GERMAN WHITE WINES appear
often in the LCBO's Vintages section, but the small selection in
the liquor board's General Purchase list is constantly disappoint-
ing. Many people are put off German wines because they believe
they're all sickly sweet. Yet while a lot of quality German wines
do have some sweetness, it's not fake and cloying, but the richness of natural sugars in the grapes.

The German wine authorities have introduced the term "Classic" to indicate wines that are dry and made from classic German grape varieties such as Riesling and Gewürztraminer. Other
terms on German wine labels include QmP (the highest quality
classification of wine) and QbA (wines of quality but not of QmP
status). Each is followed by the name of the wine region where
the grapes were grown.

Deinhard 'Classic' Riesling 2007

★ ★ ★ ½

QbA RHEINHESSEN $12.95   (60004)

"Classic" on the label of a German wine means that the wine is made
from a selected range of grape varieties in a dry style. It's designed to help
German wine escape the reputation of being too sweet. This Riesling is
quite dry, with solid and attractive fruit flavours. The crisp texture gives
a slightly spritzy sensation on your tongue. Serve it with spicy chicken or
pork, or pour as an aperitif.

NOTES

....

....

....

....

Deinhard Pinot Grigio 2007

★ ★ ★ ½

QbA BADEN $12.95   (473595)

A few years ago, Pinot Grigio (a.k.a. Pinot Gris) was on such a roll that it
seemed ready to overtake Chardonnay as the most popular white wine. It
didn't happen, but many people like its fruity, slightly spicy flavours. This
one has attractive and tangy fruitiness. It's medium bodied and refreshing,
and goes well with spicy seafood or chicken.

NOTES

....

....

....

....

Gustav Adolf Schmitt Niersteiner Spätlese/ Late Harvest 2006

★ ★ ★ ½

QmP RHEINHESSEN $10.90   (262337)

This is what too many people think *all* German white wine tastes like,
with its sweet flavours. But this one is designed to be sweet; it's a late-
harvest wine made from grapes left on the vine until late fall, when they
shrivel and have higher proportions of sugar. It's moderately sweet, with
quite luscious flavours, some complexity, and good balancing acidity.
Drink it with spicy Asian dishes or with blue cheese.

NOTES

....

....

....

....

Moselland 'Bernkasteler Kurfürstlay' Riesling 2007

★★★ ½

QbA MOSEL-SAAR-RUWER $9.95   (15875)

This Riesling comes from one of Germany's prime Riesling regions. It's off-dry and makes an excellent wine for sipping on the deck in the summer, or a year-round wine that pairs with lightly spiced Asian food, like pad Thai. It's light bodied with quite delicate flavours and the texture is crisp and clean. It makes its case for inclusion here by its versatility as an inexpensive, entry-level Riesling.

NOTES

....

....

....

....

....

HUNGARY

LITTLE REPRESENTED IN THE LCBO, Hungary has a significant position in the world of wine. Its strengths are in its whites, many made from indigenous varieties, although some producers are making wines from the internationally known grapes.

Dunavár Pinot Blanc 2006

★ ★ ★

HUNGARY $7.95   (565820)

Pinot Blanc comes in a wide range of styles. Many are, quite frankly, too delicate (lacking in taste) and light (watery). Not this one. The flavours are quite rich and vibrant and the texture is generous and mouth filling with a dose of acidity that ensures it's refreshing and crisp. It's medium bodied and quite dry, and goes well with grilled fish or seafood.

NOTES

....

....

....

....

....

ITALY

ITALY HAS A LONG HISTORY of producing white wines from indigenous grapes, but in recent years we've seen many made from what are called "international" varieties, such as Chardonnay. One variety now grown in many Italian regions is Pinot Grigio (also known as Pinot Gris). There are many mediocre Pinot Grigios, but this list identifies a number that stand out from the herd for quality and value.

The highest quality classification of Italian wines is DOCG (*Denominazione di Origine Controllata e Garantita*), which means they're made to stringent regulations and from a few specified grape varieties. So are wines in the second quality category, DOC (*Denominazione di Origine Controllata*). Wines labelled IGT (*Indicazione Geografica Tipica*) are made according to less stringent regulations and may use a wider range of grape varieties. You'll find quality and value in all these categories.

★ ★ ★ ★
Bolla Pinot Grigio 2007
IGT DELLE VENEZIE $12.00   (363622)

This Pinot Grigio comes from the Veneto region in northeast Italy and stands out for its crisp and quite lean character. Unlike many Pinot Grigios, which are low in acid and high in sweet, ripe fruit, this one is more structured and goes better with food. The flavours are solid and appealing, and the texture is refreshing. This teams well with seafood, chicken, or pasta in a light cream sauce.

NOTES

....
....
....
....

★ ★ ★
Botter 'Anna' Pinot Grigio/Chardonnay 2006
IGT VENETO $11.85   (613620)

[1-Litre Tetra Pak] Not so long ago it seemed that Pinot Grigio (a.k.a. Pinot Gris) was going to overtake Chardonnay in the popularity stakes, but Chardonnay held on. Now here they are, harnessed together, making an attractive wine for simple meals of seafood or fish. Look for clean, fresh fruit flavours, a medium body, and a crisp and refreshing texture.

NOTES

....
....
....
....

★ ★ ★
Citra Pinot Grigio 2007
IGT OSCO $7.95   (017483)

Osco is a recently designated wine region in central Italy near the Adriatic Sea. The name refers to the Oscan people who lived there in prehistoric times. This Pinot Grigio has light, fruity flavours that are nicely concentrated. It's medium bodied and has a spicy, tangy texture. Sip it alone or pour it to drink with lightly spicy Asian food, like chicken or tofu pad Thai.

NOTES

....
....
....
....

Citra Trebbiano d'Abruzzo 2007

★ ★ ★ ½

DOC TREBBIANO D'ABRUZZO $7.20   (522144)

Like many Italian wine names, this one combines a grape variety (Trebbiano) and a region (Abruzzo). It's medium bodied and has a very dry feel. Look for attractive and fairly complex fruit flavours here, and a clean and refreshing texture that makes for a good match with creamy Italian dishes. Try it with fettuccine alfredo or any pasta with a cream sauce.

NOTES

....

....

....

....

....

Collavini 'Villa Canlugo' Chardonnay 2006

★ ★ ★ ½

IGT VENEZIA GIULIA $12.15   (161034)

It would be interesting to track the proliferation of Chardonnay, as it seems to be grown everywhere. This one from northeastern Italy has quite intense aromas and flavours and a very appealing texture. There's plenty of fruitiness, but it's kept nicely in check by a good spine of acidity. This is refreshing and is good for sipping alone, but it also goes well with simply prepared roast chicken or a barbecued bird from the supermarket.

NOTES

....

....

....

....

Danzante Pinot Grigio 2006

★ ★ ★ ★ ½

IGT DELLE VENEZIE $14.40   (26906)

This is a delicious Pinot Grigio, one that really jumps out from the herd of mediocre Pinot Grigios in the LCBO and throughout the world. Danzante does seem to dance in your mouth. The texture is nimble and quite elegant, with a wonderfully refreshing burst of acidity. The flavours are lovely: complex, pure, and clean. Overall, this is very good and makes an excellent choice for lightly spiced shrimp or chicken pad Thai.

NOTES

....

....

....

....

Fazi Battaglia Verdicchio dei Castelli di Jesi Classico 2006

★ ★ ★ ★ ½

DOC VERDICCHIO DEI CASTELLI DI JESI CLASSICO

$10.95   (024422)

Fazi Battaglia packages its Verdicchio (and its Sangiovese) in a distinctive bottle that looks a bit like an elongated Coca-Cola bottle. But the contents are much, much better. There are lovely fruit flavours and there's a touch of tanginess for good measure. With its fine balance and crisp texture, this wine is ideal for many kinds of seafood and white fish.

NOTES

....
....
....
....

Folonari Pinot Grigio 2007

★ ★ ★ ★

IGT DELLE VENEZIE $14.45   (229542)

Well made, well priced, and, well . . . delicious. It's medium bodied and full of quite luscious, fresh, and zesty fruit flavours. Look for a crisp and refreshing texture and an overall excellent balance between fruit and acidity. This is the sort of wine you can sip on its own or drink with grilled white fish or roast chicken.

NOTES

....
....
....
....
....

Masi 'Masianco' 2007

★ ★ ★ ★

IGT DELLE VENEZIE $14.95   (620773)

This is a blend of the ubiquitous Pinot Grigio and the locally planted (in northern Italy's Veneto region) Verduzzo. The result is a soft texture that's quite generous and well balanced, and ripe, concentrated flavours with lovely complexity. Overall, it's a wine you can enjoy on its own or pair successfully with lightly spiced seafood, chicken, or pork.

NOTES

....
....
....
....
....

Masi 'Modello delle Venezie' 2007

★ ★ ★ ★

IGT VENEZIE $9.95   (564674)

Blending a native Italian grape (Garganega) and two international varieties, Pinot Grigio and Pinot Blanc, results in a very successful *ménage à trois* that delivers lovely ripe fruit flavours and a texture that's both smooth and refreshing. It's medium bodied and fruity, and it goes well with seafood pasta in a cream sauce, or chicken à la king.

NOTES

....

....

....

....

....

Mezzacorona Pinot Grigio 2007

★ ★ ★ ½

DOC TRENTINO $12.95   (302380)

This is a good, solid Pinot Grigio from the Trentino region in northeast Italy. It delivers attractive flavours that are fresh and quite bright, and a texture that has some substance but is also lively and refreshing. It's dry and medium bodied, and it's the sort of wine you could successfully serve with varied fish and chicken appetizers, or with dishes featuring chicken or pork.

NOTES

....

....

....

....

Mezzacorona Riserva Pinot Grigio 2006

★ ★ ★ ★ ½

DOC TRENTINO $15.85   (32714)

Here's a Riserva-level wine that's a couple of notches above your everyday Italian Pinot Grigio. To see the difference, taste the producer's entry-level Pinot Grigio (it's the review before this one) alongside it. This wine is plush and well balanced in its texture, with good structure, and has very attractive and well-defined flavours. It's a lovely wine that you can enjoy with a pork roast or with roast chicken or turkey.

NOTES

....

....

....

....

Placido Pinot Grigio 2006

★ ★ ★

IGT VENEZIE $12.60   (588897)

Count Placido, shown on the label, looks like a calm fellow as he rides past his castle and vineyards. Maybe he's just been visiting the cellar. He might be heading to enjoy a bottle of his Pinot Grigio as an aperitif or with chicken or veal in a creamy sauce. When his servant pours him a glass, he'll enjoy attractive fruity flavours and a somewhat crisper and more refreshing texture than appears in his noble neighbours' Pinot Grigios.

NOTES

Ruffino 'Lumina' Pinot Grigio 2006

★ ★ ★ ★ ½

IGT VENEZIA GIULIA $13.65   (589101)

This is a Pinot Grigio that stands out for its balance and style. The fruit is certainly there, well focused and structured, and the texture is attractive and smooth with a refreshing crispness. Everything holds together well, and it makes for a wine that you can sip alone on the deck in the summer or pair with a wide range of foods, from Thai dishes to chicken and pork.

NOTES

Ruffino Orvieto Classico 2007

★ ★ ★ ★

DOC ORVIETO CLASSICO $11.65   (31062)

The old town of Orvieto is dominated by a 13th-century cathedral (it's on the label) that's decorated with stone carvings and mosaics with grape and vine designs. It shows just how long the area has been involved in making wine. This one is medium bodied and crisp, with quite concentrated and luscious flavours. Drink it on the patio or pair it with grilled, delicate-flavoured freshwater fish, like trout.

NOTES

Santa Margherita Pinot Grigio 2006
★ ★ ★ ½
DOC VALDADIGE $16.95   (106450)

[Vintages Essential] This is a popular Pinot Grigio and the secret of its success is very likely its balance. Everything here harmonizes well. The acidity and fruit complement each other nicely, and the flavours are neither too forward nor too restrained. It makes an excellent sipping wine before a meal, but is also good with food, especially seafood.

NOTES
....
....
....
....
....

Soluna Pinot Grigio 2006
★ ★ ★
IGT VENEZIE $11.85   (614412)

[1-Litre Tetra Pak] Pinot Grigio, also known as Pinot Gris, comes in a wide range of styles, sometimes with ripe, upfront fruit, sometimes more understated. This has uncomplicated, concentrated flavours with full-on fruit, medium body and a spicy, tangy texture—the sort of wine to have with spicy seafood, chicken, or pork, maybe in an Asian style.

NOTES
....
....
....
....
....

Vivallis Pinot Grigio 2007
★ ★ ★
DOC TRENTINO $11.90   (637611)

Trentino is a wine region in the northeast of Italy, and Pinot Grigio is one of its most important white grape varieties. This version delivers solid fruit flavours, but they're moderate in intensity rather than in your face. The wine is medium bodied and nicely balanced between smoothness and crispness, and it goes very well with simple roast chicken or turkey.

NOTES
....
....
....
....

NEW ZEALAND

NEW ZEALAND IS A VERY SMALL PRODUCER of wine in global terms, but made a big name for itself in the wine world in the 1990s with Sauvignon Blancs, especially from Marlborough. They're still the core of the country's white wines, but Chardonnay and other varieties are definitely worth trying.

Babich Sauvignon Blanc 2007

★ ★ ★ ★ ½

MARLBOROUGH $17.30   (620054)

Still a family-owned company, Babich recently celebrated its 90th year at its winery just north of Auckland. The grapes for this wine come from much farther south, in the famed Marlborough region. They give the wine the classic New Zealand Sauvignon flavours of exciting and pungent fruit. It's crisp and refreshing with a smooth texture and goes wonderfully with warm goat cheese salad, or tomato and goat cheese quiche.

NOTES

....

....

....

....

Cat's Pee on a Gooseberry Bush Sauvignon Blanc 2007

★ ★ ★ ½

NEW ZEALAND $13.95   (606384)

While not all that appealing, "cat's pee on a gooseberry bush" is a classic description of Sauvignon Blanc because many show extremely pungent aromas, high acidity, and gooseberry flavours. This Sauvignon has plenty of zest and you might find hints of gooseberry in its fruit (but no cat's been near it). It's medium bodied, with a fresh, clean texture and is excellent with grilled or pan-fried white fish and lemon.

NOTES

....

....

....

....

Coopers Creek Sauvignon Blanc 2007

★ ★ ★ ★

MARLBOROUGH $16.95   (957407)

[Vintages Essential] The great white wine success story of the 1990s was Sauvignon Blanc from New Zealand's Marlborough region. This example from Coopers Creek shows what it's all about: delicious, pungent, and concentrated fruit flavours riding on a texture that's smooth, mouth filling, and zesty. This is a wine that sets you up for food. Serve it with fish and fresh lemon, or with mussels steamed in white wine.

NOTES

....

....

....

....

Kim Crawford Sauvignon Blanc 2007

★ ★ ★ ★ ½

MARLBOROUGH $19.95   (35386)

[Vintages Essential] Kim Crawford is an iconic New Zealand winemaker, one of the pioneers of the new wine industry in the country. And this is just about an iconic wine, too, with flavours and textures that are classic New Zealand Sauvignon Blanc. The fruit is rich, layered, and pungent, and the mouth feel is full and zesty. This is a fine wine to drink with grilled herbed white fish and fresh lemon.

NOTES

Monkey Bay Sauvignon Blanc 2007

★ ★ ★ ★

MARLBOROUGH $14.45   (620062)

You won't find any monkeys in New Zealand. But there really is a Monkey Bay in Marlborough, for some reason. This wine delivers very attractive flavours with pungency and depth, and a vibrant, refreshing texture. It makes a good partner for freshly shucked oysters or spicy seafood.

NOTES

Nobilo 'Regional Collection' Sauvignon Blanc 2007

★ ★ ★ ★ ½

MARLBOROUGH $15.80   (554444)

This is a popular New Zealand Sauvignon Blanc, vintage after vintage. For its price, it's a sort of classic, with wonderfully rich and pungent flavours. The texture reflects the broad seam of acidity that flows through the wine and produces a luscious tanginess that makes your mouth water in anticipation of food. This is an excellent wine for oysters or other shellfish, seafood, or fish that's been treated to a squeeze of lemon.

NOTES

Oyster Bay Chardonnay 2007

★ ★ ★ ½

MARLBOROUGH $18.95   (326728)

[Vintages Essential] The Marlborough wine region, located at the
northern end of New Zealand's South Island, is best known for Sauvignon Blanc, but also turns out fine wines from other varieties of grapes.
This medium-bodied Chardonnay has a full but clean and crisp texture,
offering rich and complex flavours. It's a versatile food wine that you can
serve with chicken, pork, fish, or seafood.

NOTES

....

....

....

....

Oyster Bay Sauvignon Blanc 2007

★ ★ ★ ★

MARLBOROUGH $18.95   (316570)

[Vintages Essential] Oyster Bay Sauvignon Blanc is well named; one of
the classic food pairings with Sauvignon Blanc is freshly shucked oysters.
The richness and acidity of the wine pick up the texture and briny flavours
of the oysters. This Sauv Blanc is quite lovely, with concentrated and pungent fruit that flows in on a tide that's crisp and refreshing. If you don't
have fresh oysters to hand, try grilled white fish with fresh lemon.

NOTES

....

....

....

....

Sacred Hill 'Whitecliff' Sauvignon Blanc 2007

★ ★ ★ ★

MARLBOROUGH $15.35   (610972)

This is a Sauvignon Blanc made in the classic Marlborough style that first
put New Zealand on the wine map. The flavours are rich, pungent, complex, and well defined, and there's a terrific seam of acidity running right
through and contributing a clean, bright, and zesty texture. It's a real palate cleanser and goes well with oysters or perhaps with a tomato and goat
cheese tart.

NOTES

....

....

....

....

Villa Maria 'Private Bin' Sauvignon Blanc 2007

★ ★ ★ ★

MARLBOROUGH $16.30   (426601)

Villa Maria is a well-established New Zealand winery that I used to visit when I was a teenager living in Auckland. It's now transformed from a small local winery to a global exporter, thanks to wines like this Sauvignon Blanc. It delivers concentrated and nicely defined flavours, and a rich and zesty texture that picks up the natural acidity of the grape. Delicious stuff and great with grilled white fish with a squeeze of lemon.

NOTES

....

....

....

....

....

ONTARIO

WHITE WINES ARE SOME OF THE BEST produced in Ontario. The cool growing conditions allow the grapes to ripen while achieving the levels of acidity they need to be crisp and refreshing. The most successful white varieties in the province include Riesling, Chardonnay, Sauvignon Blanc, and Gewürztraminer.

"VQA" (Vintners Quality Alliance) on an Ontario wine, followed by the name of a wine region, means that the wine was made mainly or wholly from grapes grown in that region and that the wine was tested and tasted for quality. Such wines can only be made from grapes grown in Ontario. For a quality Ontario wine, look for the VQA symbol.

Non-VQA wines in the LCBO's Canada and Ontario sections are usually "Cellared in Canada" wines, which means they're blends of a small amount of Ontario wine and a high percentage of foreign wine. Cellared in Canada wines are not included in this book because their range and volume vary according to the grape harvest in Ontario.

Angels Gate Gewürztraminer 2006

★ ★ ★

VQA NIAGARA PENINSULA $15.95   (58594)

Angels Gate is so-named because the property at one time belonged to
a religious order of missionary sisters. (It was later a mink farm, too, but
"Minkgate" sounds like a political scandal.) This is an appealing Gewürztraminer with a round, smooth, fat texture that delivers delicate but pungent flavours characteristic of the variety. Off-dry and zesty, it's a good
choice for spicy (maybe Thai-influenced) seafood, chicken, and pork dishes.

NOTES

....

....

....

....

Birchwood Estate Gewürztraminer/Riesling 2006

★ ★ ★

VQA NIAGARA PENINSULA $10.95   (572156)

Birchwood is one of Niagara's smaller wineries, located near the shore of
Lake Ontario. This attractive blend is a slightly sweet wine with intense
and pungent flavours. It's medium bodied, with a refreshing, crisp texture that balances the hint of sweetness and makes this a good food wine.
Serve it with spicy barbecued shrimp or with pork and applesauce.

NOTES

....

....

....

....

Cave Spring Chardonnay Musqué 2005

★ ★ ★ ½

VQA NIAGARA PENINSULA $15.95   (246579)

[Vintages Essential] Chardonnay Musqué is a variant of the Chardonnay
grape that gives its wine a perfumed, spicy, or musky character. You can
smell and taste it here in a very delicate form: The flavours are more pungent and edgy than straight Chardonnay. It feels quite full and round in
the mouth, but the good seam of acidity lends some tanginess, making it
a nice choice for well-seasoned chicken or pork.

NOTES

....

....

....

....

....

Cave Spring Dry Riesling 2006

★ ★ ★ ½   VQA NIAGARA PENINSULA $13.85   (233635)

Cave Spring quickly established a reputation for Riesling, and it's still among the best producers in Ontario. Its Rieslings tend to be stylish and complex, and they go beautifully with food. This one has a crisp but quite generous texture that's complemented with lovely fruit flavours. It's dry and refreshing, and medium bodied. You can sip it as an aperitif, but it has the stuff to go with smoked chicken or pork tenderloin.

NOTES

....

....

....

....

Cave Spring 'Estate Bottled' Chardonnay 2004

★ ★ ★ ★ ½   VQA BEAMSVILLE BENCH $19.95   (256552)

[Vintages Essential] Wine writers occasionally refer to the ABC movement—meaning Anything But Chardonnay—because, supposedly, many people are tired of the wine. They should taste this. It's rich and elegant, with solid fruit flavours that fill your mouth with liquid pleasure. It approaches full bodied, has a luxurious texture, and goes with turkey, rich chicken, or pork dishes.

NOTES

....

....

....

....

Cave Spring 'Estate Bottled' Riesling 2006

★ ★ ★ ★ ½   VQA BEAMSVILLE BENCH $17.80   (286377)

[Vintages Essential] Beamsville Bench is one of more than a dozen sub-appellations (or sub-regions) that the Niagara Peninsula wine region has been divided into. It might be a bit confusing for consumers, but what's *not* confusing is this only just off-dry Riesling. It delivers delicious, intense flavours on a texture that's brisk and clean and makes you want to eat. So eat. Pair this with spicy seafood or smoked salmon.

NOTES

....

....

....

....

★ ★ ★ ½

Château des Charmes Aligoté 2006

VQA NIAGARA PENINSULA $13.45   (284950)

Aligoté is a little-known grape variety. It's from Burgundy, where most of the white wine is made from Chardonnay. This example has the crisp acidity and clean, refreshing aftertaste that are characteristic of the variety, making it ideal for seafood and shellfish. It has quite well-defined and concentrated flavours. Try it with mussels steamed in white wine and garlic.

NOTES

....
....
....
....
....

★ ★ ★ ★

Château des Charmes Chardonnay 2006

VQA NIAGARA-ON-THE-LAKE $11.45   (056754)

Chardonnay is sometimes called "the winemaker's grape" because it's more neutral than most varieties and allows the winemaker to put her/his stamp on it more clearly. This one is made in a very attractive style, with balance as one of its main assets. The fruit is well defined and concentrated, the texture fairly plush and refreshing, and it has a clean finish. It's a great choice for many foods, including chicken, white fish, and seafood.

NOTES

....
....
....
....

★ ★ ★ ½

Château des Charmes Riesling 2006

VQA NIAGARA-ON-THE-LAKE $12.45   (061499)

Niagara-on-the-Lake is one of several smaller wine regions (sub-appellations) within the larger Niagara Peninsula region that can now be shown on wine labels, as long as all the grapes in the wine were grown there. These Riesling grapes have produced a very attractive, medium-bodied, dry wine with a texture that's smooth and crisp, with focused fruity flavours. Drink it with roast chicken or pork, or with seafood.

NOTES

....
....
....
....

Château des Charmes Sauvignon Blanc 2006

★ ★ ★ ★

VQA NIAGARA-ON-THE-LAKE $15.95   (391300)

Niagara-on-the-Lake is one of the sub-appellations (wine regions) within the larger Niagara Peninsula wine region. This Sauvignon Blanc is really lovely, with lively, bright, and substantial flavours and an exuberant and refreshing texture. It's dry and medium bodied and is an excellent wine to serve with grilled white fish and freshly squeezed lemon.

NOTES

....

....

....

....

....

Dan Aykroyd Chardonnay 2006

★ ★ ★ ½

VQA ONTARIO $14.55   (53934)

A wine labelled "VQA Ontario" means that the producer can source grapes from anywhere in the province, and it usually means the grapes have in fact come from more than one Ontario wine region. This is a quite attractive Chardonnay, with nicely defined and reasonably complex flavours, and a smooth, refreshing texture. It's dry and medium bodied, and you can't go wrong serving it with chicken, pork, or turkey.

NOTES

....

....

....

....

Henry of Pelham Dry Riesling 2006

★ ★ ★ ★

VQA NIAGARA PENINSULA $13.25   (268375)

Riesling has led the way with screw caps, first in New Zealand and Australia, then elsewhere. The seal captures the freshness you want in the variety, and Henry of Pelham has done that. This dry Riesling is packed with delicious flavour and delivers a mouth-filling and zesty texture. It's a great choice for sipping on the deck or before dinner, and it also goes with spicy seafood, chicken, or pork dishes.

NOTES

....

....

....

....

Henry of Pelham Non-Oaked Chardonnay 2006

★ ★ ★

VQA NIAGARA PENINSULA $13.25 (291211)

Some say "non-oaked," some say "unoaked," but both mean that the wine was made and aged in stainless steel so as to preserve the purity of the fruit flavours. It works here, all right. The flavours are substantial but nuanced and delicate, and the texture is clean and refreshing. It's a natural for roast chicken or pork and for simply prepared white fish. This wine is also available in a half-bottle size (375 mL) for $6.95 (598946).

NOTES

....

....

....

....

Henry of Pelham Reserve Chardonnay 2006

★ ★ ★ ½

VQA NIAGARA PENINSULA $14.95 (252833)

The word "Reserve" has no legal meaning in most wine laws, but it's generally an indication that the producer thinks it is better quality than a non-Reserve wine. This one from Henry of Pelham is a notch or two up and delivers some finesse and style. The flavours are delicate and complex, and the texture is generous, round, and refreshing. It's dry and medium weight, and a natural for roast chicken.

NOTES

....

....

....

....

Henry of Pelham Reserve Riesling 2006

★ ★ ★ ½

VQA SHORT HILLS BENCH $14.95 (283291)

From selected areas of Riesling vines on Henry of Pelham's own estate in the Short Hills Bench sub-appellation of Niagara, this is fairly dry and delivers very appealing fruit flavours. A bit more than medium-bodied, it has a very crisp and clean texture, and goes with a variety of fish and seafood dishes. Why not drink this with a bowl of steamed mussels and a plate of fries?

NOTES

....

....

....

....

Henry of Pelham Sauvignon Blanc 2006

★ ★ ★

VQA NIAGARA PENINSULA $14.95   (430546)

[Vintages Essential] Henry of Pelham is better known for its red wines, but it also turns out many fine whites, as the entries in this book show. This Sauvignon Blanc has all the crispness of texture and brightness of fruit you look for in this variety. You'll find lots of lively, vibrant flavours and aromas here. It's dry and medium bodied and goes well with grilled or pan-fried white fish with fresh lemon.

NOTES

....

....

....

....

Hillebrand 'Artist Series' Gewürztraminer 2006

★ ★ ★ ★

VQA NIAGARA PENINSULA $10.95   (554378)

Hillebrand has long supported the arts—their summer concerts are sell-outs—and for their Artist Series they commissioned works for the labels. The dog playing sax on this one might well have just tasted the wine. It's all Gewürztraminer but in a restrained style, rather than the perfumed, blowsy Gewürztraminers that often dominate food. Look for rich, spicy, pungent fruitiness and a refreshing texture, and pair it with spicy chicken or seafood.

NOTES

....

....

....

....

Inniskillin Chardonnay 2006

★ ★ ★

VQA NIAGARA PENINSULA $10.95   (66266)

Inniskillin winery was named for Inniskillin Farm that, after the War of 1812, was a land grant to a colonel in the Royal Inniskilling Fusiliers. This is a straightforward, uncomplicated Chardonnay with well-defined flavours. It's medium bodied, with a crisp, refreshing texture—the sort of wine you can sip in the afternoon or enjoy with a chicken sandwich.

NOTES

....

....

....

Inniskillin 'Reserve Series' Chardonnay 2006

★ ★ ★ ½

VQA NIAGARA PENINSULA $15.50   (317768)

When Inniskillin got a licence to make wine in 1974, it was the first
new winery in Ontario since Prohibition ended in the province in 1927.
This more recent Chardonnay is well made, with appealing fruit flavours.
It's medium bodied, with a texture that's both smooth and a little juicy,
and it goes very well with roast chicken, grilled or pan-fried white fish,
and seafood.

NOTES

Jackson-Triggs 'Proprietors' Reserve' Gewürztraminer 2006

★ ★ ★ ½

VQA NIAGARA PENINSULA $12.25   (526269)

Jackson-Triggs is one of the biggest brands in the LCBO, and "Proprietors'
Reserve" is one of its premium lines. This Gewürztraminer is made in a
very appealing style. The flavours are nicely framed and solid, but they
have a certain delicacy, while the texture is both mouth filling and spicy.
There's a hint of clean bitterness that you often get with this variety and
that I like. Drink this with spicy seafood or with Thai dishes.

NOTES

Jackson-Triggs 'Proprietors' Reserve' Sauvignon Blanc 2006

★ ★ ★ ½

VQA NIAGARA PENINSULA $13.95   (58438)

Sauvignon Blanc is one of the white grapes that do well in Niagara's cool
growing conditions, which bring out the acidity typical of the variety. You
see it in this appealing example, which is dry and medium bodied, with a
crisp, refreshing texture that suits freshly shucked oysters or grilled white
fish. The flavours are bright and vibrant and quite concentrated.

NOTES

Konzelmann Pinot Blanc 2007

★ ★ ★ ½

VQA NIAGARA PENINSULA $10.95   (219279)

Konzelmann Estate Winery is located near Niagara-on-the-Lake, close to the shore of Lake Ontario. This Pinot Blanc (the label also calls it *Weissburgunder*, the grape's name in Germany) delivers attractive and quite intense fruity flavours, with a round, smooth but refreshing texture. This is a good sipping wine, and it will also go well with chicken and pork tenderloin.

NOTES

....

....

....

....

....

Konzelmann Vidal 2006

★ ★ ★

VQA ONTARIO $9.95   (203836)

Vidal is a much-maligned variety when used for table wines, although it's widely used in Ontario for icewine. Konzelmann's Vidal is a semi-sweet white that has quite rich and complex fruitiness complemented by a round, smooth texture with enough acidity to cut through the sweetness. Its low alcohol (11.5 percent) makes this a good wine to sip in the summer or drink with spicy chicken or pork.

NOTES

....

....

....

....

Legends Gewürztraminer 2006

★ ★ ★ ★

VQA NIAGARA PENINSULA $13.95   (390211)

Legends Estate Winery is located close to the shore of Lake Ontario. This is a quite delightful Gewürztraminer with all the character of the variety, but in a fairly light and delicate style. The pungent and sweet fruit flavours are well defined, though, and the texture is quite rich and very zesty. This is an excellent choice for lightly spiced Thai pork, chicken, and tofu dishes.

NOTES

....

....

....

....

Mike Weir Chardonnay 2006

★ ★ ★ ★

VQA NIAGARA PENINSULA $15.95   (26)

[Vintages Essential] Yes, 26 is the product code number, not Mike's score around nine holes. The Chardonnay plays well right through the course. It drives off with quite intense and complex flavours and hits the fairway with a fairly generous texture offset by good acidity. It's as dry as a summer day on the links and medium bodied. You'll be popular putting this out when you're serving roast chicken or grilled salmon.

NOTES

....

....

....

....

Pelee Island 'eco trail' Chardonnay/Auxerrois 2007

★ ★ ★

VQA ONTARIO $9.90   (591719)

This is a white blend that includes the well-known Chardonnay and the less-known Auxerrois, which is grown widely in Alsace. Auxerrois tends to be low in acid and quite fruity, and you can taste and feel its influence in this wine. It's fruit-sweet in flavour and quite plump and mouth filling in texture, but with a balancing dose of acidity. This goes well with slightly spicy dishes (like Thai food).

NOTES

....

....

....

....

Peninsula Ridge 'Inox' Chardonnay 2006

★ ★ ★ ★

VQA NIAGARA PENINSULA $13.15   (594200)

This is an unoaked Chardonnay (not aged in oak barrels) from Peninsula Ridge winemaker Jean-Pierre Colas, who made his reputation in France's Chablis region, where the most common wine is . . . unoaked Chardonnay. Look for clean, pure flavours. It's almost full bodied, with a generous texture, and it's excellent with pork, chicken, and white fish.

NOTES

....

....

....

....

....

Peninsula Ridge Sauvignon Blanc 2006

★ ★ ★ ★

VQA NIAGARA PENINSULA $14.95   (53678)

Peninsula Ridge was the first winery where I tasted an Ontario Sauvignon Blanc that I thought was stunning. It's vintage variable, but this one is full of Sauvignon character, with clean and pungent fruit flavours, a fairly full texture that's quite high in refreshing acidity, and a long, clean finish. Drink it with the usual suspects—freshly shucked oysters—or with battered white fish, tartar sauce, and chips.

NOTES

....

....

....

....

Stoney Ridge Riesling 2007

★ ★ ★ ½

VQA NIAGARA PENINSULA $12.10   (287334)

One of Niagara's older wineries, Stoney Ridge makes a wide range of wines, many of them very good value. This is an off-dry Riesling that you can happily sip on the patio in the summer, serve as an aperitif before dinner in the winter, or drink with spicy seafood or chicken dishes. It has solid yet delicate flavours and a quite juicy, crisp texture.

NOTES

....

....

....

....

Strewn Semi-Dry Riesling 2006

★ ★ ★

VQA NIAGARA PENINSULA $11.95   (616599)

The name of this winery has no relation to wine, location, or the owners' names. They were simply looking for a word that was pithy and neutral, and "strewn" fitted the bill. This off-dry Riesling tastes more dry than off, but it delivers solid and quite attractive flavours on the zesty, crisp texture that you expect from Riesling. Sip it by itself or serve with roast chicken or with smoked salmon on a bagel.

NOTES

....

....

....

....

Trius Riesling Dry 2006

★ ★ ★ ½

VQA NIAGARA PENINSULA $13.95   (303792)

With so many good-quality and good-value Rieslings around, it's sad that the variety isn't more popular. Is it because many people still associate it with older-style sweet wines? This one is bone dry and full of lovely vibrant fruit flavours, and has a lively, crisp texture. It's medium bodied and is an excellent choice for slightly spiced seafood or chicken dishes.

NOTES

....

....

....

....

....

PORTUGAL

PORTUGAL DOESN'T SHOW VERY BRIGHTLY on the radar of Ontario wine drinkers, and when it does, it's more for the reds than the whites. The best-known Portuguese white is Vinho Verde, a fruity, spritzy wine that's meant to be drunk young, but there are other interesting whites made from indigenous grapes.

Official wine regions are indicated by DOC (*Denominação de Origem Controlada*).

★ ★ ★
Aliança Vinho Verde Branco 2007

DOC VINHO VERDE $8.45   (75663)

This Vinho Verde has quite fruity flavours and the vibrant and spritzy texture that you expect from the wine. It's not complicated, it's not demanding, you don't have to think about it. Just open the bottle (why doesn't this have a screw cap?) and sit back and sip it while you read or talk on the deck in the summer. The low alcohol (9 percent) means you can enjoy it longer in the sun. You can also enjoy it with light appetizers.

NOTES

....

....

....

....

★ ★ ★
Aveleda Vinho Verde 2007

DOC VINHO VERDE $8.45   (5322)

Vinho verde translates as "green wine," but not in the sense of being unripe. It means the wine is young (and should be drunk like that). There's a little fizziness in the bottle and, combined with the vibrant, fresh fruitiness of the flavours, it makes for a refreshing white to sip during the summer. It's fairly dry and has low alcohol (10.5 percent)—and that also helps in the summer heat. Drink it alone or with light, spicy appetizers.

NOTES

....

....

....

....

★ ★ ★ ½
Mateus 'Signature' 2006

DOC DOURO $8.45   (308635)

If you're old enough, you probably remember Mateus rosé, the fruity pink wine from Portugal that came in the slightly funky bottle that made such a great candle holder. You've changed, and so has the wine. The rosé has been reinvented and now there's this crisp and fruity white that makes a very pleasant sipping wine in summer and a nice drink to have with grilled seafood. Honestly, you won't go wrong with this.

NOTES

....

....

....

....

SOUTH AFRICA

SOUTH AFRICA'S WINE REGIONS ARE MOSTLY WARM, which makes you think red wine. But they produce many very good-quality whites, too. The most popular variety used to be Chenin Blanc, but over the last ten years others (especially Chardonnay and Sauvignon Blanc) have become more important.

A wine from a designated wine region in South Africa is called a "Wine of Origin," and bottles of South African wine display the region clearly. In this list, the wine region is shown after the letters "wo" (Wine of Origin).

Drostdy-Hof Chardonnay 2007

★ ★ ★ ½

WO WESTERN CAPE $9.65   (343202)

The producer's name reminds us that the Dutch started the wine industry in South Africa. As early as the 1600s, Dutch ships would stop on the way to the East Indies (now Indonesia) to pick up supplies of wine for their crews to help stave off scurvy. Drink this Chardonnay for health or pleasure. It has good fruit flavours, a smooth texture, and a light-to-medium body. Enjoy it with a chicken burger.

NOTES

....

....

....

....

Flat Roof Manor Pinot Grigio 2007

★ ★ ★ ½

WO STELLENBOSCH $11.95   (27128)

There's a cat (it looks like a Siamese) walking on the flat roof, and the label reads, "So many lives, so little time." It doesn't make a lot of sense, but the wine is quite attractive. This is a well-made Pinot Grigio with some complexity to the flavours and a nicely balanced texture. It's dry and medium bodied and goes well with lightly spiced Thai dishes and grilled seafood.

NOTES

....

....

....

....

KWV Chardonnay 2007

★ ★ ★ ½

WO WESTERN CAPE $9.95   (304360)

There's a world of Chardonnays out there in a seemingly infinite number of styles. Chardonnay is a fairly neutral variety that enables winemakers to put their personal imprint on it. This is a straightforward, fruity Chard that drives a middle line, with good solid fruit and a well-balanced texture. It will offend no one and please many. Serve it alone or with chicken or pork.

NOTES

....

....

....

....

Nederburg Sauvignon Blanc 2007

★ ★ ★ ½

WO COASTAL REGION $11.45   (382713)

Nederburg is an established (it's over two centuries old) and big (production is about 13 million bottles a year) South African wine producer. Although age is sometimes seen as an advantage, size can be a problem, but the company keeps quality up. This Sauvignon Blanc is zesty and refreshing, with good, clean flavours. It's made for food, so pair it with seafood or fish with a squeeze of lemon.

NOTES
....
....
....

Oracle Sauvignon Blanc 2006

★ ★ ★

WO WESTERN CAPE $10.95   (36764)

The label refers to the "oracle of the wind," and whatever that means, there must have been some cool offshore breezes blowing through the vineyards where the grapes for this wine grew. Although it doesn't have the raciness of some Sauvignon Blancs, it will please wine drinkers averse to higher levels of acidity. You get pretty flavours, a solid and crisp texture, and a decent finish. It goes well with grilled white fish.

NOTES
....
....
....

Two Oceans Sauvignon Blanc 2007

★ ★ ★ ★

WO WESTERN CAPE $9.65   (340380)

The two oceans involved here are the Atlantic and the Indian, and where they meet (the point shifts seasonally) off South Africa's coast, they create breezes that blow onto the land and cool the vines. This is quite a lovely Sauvignon Blanc, with well-defined and nicely concentrated flavours and a crisp, clean texture. Enjoy it with warm goat cheese salad or with white fish or seafood.

NOTES
....
....
....
....

SPAIN

SPAIN IS BEST KNOWN FOR ITS RED WINES and its sparkling wine called Cava (which is listed in this book's Sparkling Wine & Champagne section). Much of the white table wine that Spain produces is consumed locally and never reaches international markets. However, that's changing as some of the larger wineries, like Torres, occasionally make white wines available in the Vintages section. Hopefully, some of these will make their way to the General Purchase list.

Marqués de Riscal 2007

★ ★ ★ ½

DO RUEDA $12.30   (036822)

This is an attractive blend that's excellent for sipping on the patio or before a meal. Serve it with grilled or pan-fried white fish or roast chicken. It's dry and medium bodied, with attractive and fairly concentrated fruit flavours. The texture is appealing, with richness from the fruit that's complemented by a refreshing crispness. It's great by itself or with food.

NOTES

....

....

....

....

ARGENTINA

ARGENTINA IS THE WORLD'S FIFTH-LARGEST wine producer, but it's still a bit of a sleeper. Although we see more and more quality and high-value wines from there, we haven't seen half of what Argentina can do. Wine producers there (most located in the high-altitude Mendoza region) make superlative reds and whites, but it's the reds that are starting to get the attention. Besides Cabernet Sauvignon, Merlot, and Shiraz/Syrah, there's Malbec, which has become Argentina's signature variety. Made in big and robust styles, it's a natural for beef, which just happens to be another major product of Argentina.

Argento Malbec 2007

★ ★ ★

MENDOZA $10.10   (591693)

This is a simple, uncomplicated Malbec. It expresses the intense fruitiness of the variety, but doesn't strive to attain the high levels of complexity it's capable of. Instead, you get a well-made, easy-drinking red that's full of sweet fruit flavour. The texture is quite rich, with some moderate tannins. You can drink this with burgers or grilled spicy sausages. To dial back the fruitiness, chill it down a little.

NOTES

....

....

....

....

Finca Flichman 'Misterio' Malbec 2007

★ ★ ★ ½

MENDOZA $9.90   (28803)

This is 100 percent Malbec and another example of the quality Argentina produces at the entry level. It's all New World in style, with upfront fruitiness and an easygoing and generous texture that will appeal to many consumers looking for good-quality reds to go with barbecues and casual meals. It's dry, somewhat tannic, medium- to full-bodied, and has enough complexity to raise it above others at this price.

NOTES

....

....

....

....

Funky Llama Shiraz 2007

★ ★ ★

MENDOZA $9.90   (614685)

Quite a few wineries keep llamas around, and while the *crias* (baby llamas) are cute, the adults aren't the most attractive of animals. This Shiraz is best enjoyed young, too. It's medium bodied and dry, with light to medium tannins. It's quite well balanced and has a good tangy texture. This is a versatile red that goes well with barbecued or broiled red meats and burgers.

NOTES

....

....

....

....

Lurton Cabernet Sauvignon 2006

★ ★ ★ ½

MENDOZA $10.95   (614644)

The Lurton brothers make wine successfully in a number of countries, including Argentina. This Cabernet Sauvignon has upfront fruity flavours with a core of ripe sweetness. The texture is full and slightly tangy, with drying tannins. Medium-bodied and dry, it's a good choice if you're cooking ribs in barbecue sauce, juicy burgers, or a spicy red meat dish.

NOTES

....
....
....
....
....

Masi Passo Doble 'Tupungato' 2006

★ ★ ★ ★

MENDOZA $14.95   (620880)

The globalization of the wine industry includes not only "flying winemakers" but also wandering wineries. This flavour-filled red blend of Italy's Corvina and Argentina's Malbec grapes is made in Argentina by Masi, an Italian winery. Look for layers of complex, rich flavours, and a tangy, tannic, well-structured texture. It's slightly more than medium bodied, is dry, and goes perfectly with rich red meat dishes.

NOTES

....
....
....
....

Pascual Toso Malbec 2007

★ ★ ★ ★ ½

MENDOZA $12.95   (35170)

Pascual Toso was founded in the late 19th century by an Italian immigrant to Argentina. Today it produces a range of excellent wines, including this 100 percent Malbec. The flavours here are complex, concentrated, and layered, and they're complemented by a generous and juicy texture. The wine is medium bodied, dry and has firm tannins. Drink this as they would in Argentina, with roasted or grilled red meats.

NOTES

....
....
....
....

Pascual Toso Merlot 2000

★ ★ ★ ★

MENDOZA $12.95   (35188)

The richness of this lovely Merlot will come as a surprise the first time you taste it. The fruit-forward flavours are dense and defined, and the texture is smooth and mouth filling. It's on the fat side (low in acidity), so if acidity bothers you, try this. It's dry, medium- to full-bodied, and moderately tannic, and it goes nicely with well-seasoned steak and other red meats.

NOTES

Trapiche Reserve Malbec 2006

★ ★ ★ ½

MENDOZA $12.05   (614651)

Trapiche (pronounced *tra-PEE-chay*) owns more than a thousand hectares of vines in Mendoza, Argentina's major wine region, and much is planted in Malbec, which has become the country's signature grape variety. This example is medium bodied, dry, and juicy textured, with quite concentrated flavours. It's not too complex, and it goes well with barbecued red meats and chicken.

NOTES

AUSTRALIA

AUSTRALIA IS A REAL POWERHOUSE FOR RED WINE, and Australian Shiraz has dominated New World red wine exports for years. But although Shiraz is king, other red varieties are very important, notably Cabernet Sauvignon, Merlot, and Pinot Noir.

The most common geographical designation for Australian wine is South Eastern Australia. This isn't a state but a mega-zone that includes more than 90 percent of the country's wine production and most of its wine regions. The best-known smaller wine regions include Barossa Valley, McLaren Vale, and Hunter Valley, all of which are represented in this book.

Angove's 'Red Belly Black' Shiraz 2006

★ ★ ★ ★

SOUTH AUSTRALIA $16.95   (58669)

Australia has most of the world's venomous snakes, including the red belly black. Angove's took a chance on using it for their Shiraz, and it's paid off, as the wine has proved successful around the world. It's rich, quite opulent, and smooth textured, with concentrated and layered flavours, and very good balance. Enjoy this with grilled lamb chops or any red meat.

NOTES

....
....
....
....
....

Angus the Bull Cabernet Sauvignon 2006

★ ★ ★ ★ ★

AUSTRALIA $18.95   (602615)

Now and again a wine stands out from the herd, and Angus is one of those. It's a dense, generous, juicy mouthful of complex flavour—sweet but not jammy—and it's full bodied and lightly tannic. You'll have no beef with the claim that Angus is great with . . . beef. But don't be cowed by this and don't let me steer you away from serving Angus with other red meats.

NOTES

....
....
....
....
....

Banrock Station Shiraz/Cabernet Sauvignon 2007

★ ★ ★ ½

SOUTH EASTERN AUSTRALIA $20.90   (526996)

[1.5 Litre] The big bottle (equal to two standard wine bottles) makes it a good choice for a party or barbecue. The wine is a good choice, too! It's a straightforward, Shiraz-dominant blend whose fruity flavour and tangy texture are sure to go down well with a wide range of wine drinkers. Look for intense flavours of sweet, ripe fruit. It goes well with ribs, burgers, and grilled red meats.

NOTES

....
....
....

Banrock Station Shiraz/Mataro 2007

★ ★ ★ ★

SOUTH EASTERN AUSTRALIA $10.95   (555771)

The Mataro grape variety is also known as Mourvèdre, and it contributes dense flavours and colour to wine. So does Shiraz, and the combination is pretty good, especially at this price. You'll experience really sweet fruit—not sugary or jammy sweetness, but the sort that comes with ripeness. It's dry with light tannins and goes well with rich meat like lamb or venison.

NOTES

....

....

....

....

....

Black Opal Cabernet/Merlot 2006

★ ★ ★ ½

SOUTH EASTERN AUSTRALIA $14.95   (351890)

They blended Cabernet and Merlot together for centuries in Bordeaux, and called it Bordeaux (or after one of the Bordeaux appellations). It wasn't until New World wines, with their emphasis on grape varieties, became popular, that Cab-Merlot became such a familiar term. This example is quite lovely, with solid, well-defined flavours and a mid-weight, smooth texture. It's dry and fairly tannic, and goes well with red meats or with aged cheeses.

NOTES

....

....

....

....

Black Opal Cabernet Sauvignon 2007

★ ★ ★ ★

SOUTH EASTERN AUSTRALIA $14.55   (343293)

Canadian tourists to Australia often bring back opals, but this is one they needn't bother packing because it's already here. This is all Cabernet Sauvignon, with quite delicious and concentrated fruit and a mouth-filling and almost opulent texture. It's dry with tannins you feel on your gums and cheeks, and makes a great wine to have with a pepper steak or well-seasoned lamb chops.

NOTES

....

....

....

d'Arenberg 'd'Arry's Original' Shiraz/Grenache 2005

★ ★ ★ ★ ½

MCLAREN VALE $19.95   (942904)

[Vintages Essential] You find a lot of wines from the south of France that feature this blend, but this is in a no-nonsense New World style that's quite different. It features intense and complex fruit flavours that are solid from front to back and leave a long finish. It's medium bodied, dry with a little tannic grip, and the texture is rich and tangy. This is a perfect match for a well-seasoned rack of lamb, grilled medium-rare at most.

NOTES

....

....

....

Deakin Estate Merlot 2004

★ ★ ★ ★

VICTORIA $12.00   (577395)

Victoria's wine regions are generally among Australia's cooler-climate areas, and this Merlot is typical. Unlike reds from warmer regions, which tend to be riper and fuller flavoured, this Merlot has concentrated but controlled flavours and decent structure. It's medium bodied and dry, with light tannins, and it goes well with spicy beef, chicken, or pork kebabs.

NOTES

....

....

....

....

....

De Bortoli 'Deen De Bortoli' Vat 8 Shiraz 2006

★ ★ ★ ★

SOUTH EASTERN AUSTRALIA $15.95   (621649)

This is a nice change from many Shirazes at this price level. It has all the full-on flavour you expect of Shiraz, but it's quite well structured and has a bright, juicy texture that sets it up for food. It's dry and medium bodied, and although it has quite high alcohol (14 percent), there's no sign of it in the flavour or texture. Drink this with grilled meats such as lamb and veal.

NOTES

....

....

....

....

De Bortoli 'Deen De Bortoli' Vat 9 Cabernet Sauvignon 2004

★ ★ ★ ★

SOUTH EASTERN AUSTRALIA $15.95   (17467)

The "Deen de Bortoli" line is named for the late son of the company's founders, who opened the winery in 1928. Like Deen, the wines are said to be "full of character and down to earth." The Vat 9 (a nice change from bin numbers) is a complex, dry Cabernet with attractive fruit flavours. It's medium bodied, nicely tannic, and it goes well with grilled or roasted red meats.

NOTES

....

....

....

....

Greg Norman Cabernet/Merlot 2005

★ ★ ★ ★ ½

LIMESTONE COAST $24.95   (552075)

[Vintages Essential] When you play golf, you not only want a good result, but you want to do it with style. This goal, which so many of us fail to achieve, seems to lie behind golfer Greg Norman's wines. They have real substance, notably in the full fruit flavours and generous texture, but the substance is not achieved at the expense of character and style. This medium-weight blend is attractive all the way through and an excellent choice for red meats.

NOTES

....

....

....

....

Greg Norman Shiraz 2005

★ ★ ★ ★

LIMESTONE COAST $24.95   (575092)

[Vintages Essential] Another of the handful of pro-golfer wines, this Shiraz scores well above par. That might not be a good thing in golf, but it is in wine. It has quite saturated flavours that are bold and broad without being jammy. The texture is smooth, round, and mouth filling, with a nice level of acidity, and the tannins are there but not too prominent. In all, it's nicely balanced and goes well with grilled or roasted red meats.

NOTES

....

....

Hardys 'Bankside' Shiraz 2005

★ ★ ★ ½

SOUTH AUSTRALIA $14.95   (436022)

[Vintages Essential] This is a Shiraz that lies in a comfortable position between jammy wines and those that are more restrained and highly structured. It's quite stylish and delivers ripe flavours with a core of fruit sweetness. It's dry with quite gripping tannins, and has a full and generous texture that coats your mouth with flavour. Serve this with a rich meal, like lamb stew and sweet root vegetables.

NOTES
....
....
....
....

Hardys Reserve Cabernet Sauvignon 2005

★ ★ ★ ½

AUSTRALIA $14.15   (24612)

[1-Litre Tetra Pak] Most wine in Australia is sold in boxes, but it's taken longer for us to catch on that you can get decent wine in a format other than a bottle. Light- to medium-bodied, this offers rich, dark berry fruit with a warm finish. Straightforward and easy drinking, it comes in sensible packaging for taking on trips and for folks concerned with the environment. This is a good price for a litre of wine that goes well with everything from pizza to steak.

NOTES
....
....
....
....

Hardys 'Stamp of Australia' Cabernet/Merlot 2006

★ ★ ★ ½

SOUTH EASTERN AUSTRALIA $10.95   (582395)

The Cab-Merlot blend, which first achieved success in Bordeaux, is now made virtually everywhere. This example stands out from many at a similar price, delivering full ripe fruit flavours with moderate complexity, and a quite rich and juicy texture. It's medium bodied and dry, with virtually no perceptible tannins. This is the sort of easy drinking red you can sip on its own or serve with a range of meat-based dishes.

NOTES
....
....
....

★ ★ ★ ★ **Hardys 'Stamp of Australia' Shiraz/ Cabernet Sauvignon 2007**

SOUTH EASTERN AUSTRALIA $10.95 (338012)

The labels of the "Stamp" series wines show older Australian stamps, and the one on this bottle has a denomination of a halfpenny. Mailing a letter for that price seems as good a deal as this wine. It has a lot of substance, first in the solid, quite complex flavours, and then in the tangy and bold texture. It's dry with light tannins, and goes well with spicy beef dishes.

NOTES
....
....
....
....
....

★ ★ ★ ★ **Jacob's Creek Reserve Shiraz 2005**

SOUTH AUSTRALIA $17.45 (665471)

Jacob's Creek is an actual creek that meanders through the Barossa wine region. It's undistinguished as bodies of water go, but the little winery on its bank that first produced wine in 1850 *did* acquire distinction. This Reserve Shiraz is a bold effort, with big flavours of ripe fruit. It's slightly more than medium bodied, is tangy textured, and goes wonderfully with grilled lamb, of course.

NOTES
....
....
....

★ ★ ★ ½ **Kangaroo Springs Shiraz 2005**

RIVERLAND/BAROSSA $11.15 (456194)

I suppose a kangaroo springs, but it also jumps and hops. As Australian wines in the LCBO tend to occupy higher price levels, and wines from other countries fill in at the lower levels, it's good to find a well-made and inexpensive Australian Shiraz. This dry, fruit-forward red has well-defined and concentrated flavours and a clean and refreshing texture. It's a natural for barbecued red meats.

NOTES
....
....
....
....

★ ★ ★ ★ ★

Katnook Estate 'Founder's Block' Cabernet Sauvignon 2005

COONAWARRA $18.00   (620070)

Coonawarra, in South Australia, has earned a reputation for fine Cabernet Sauvignon. To see why, try this one, made by Katnook's winemaker, Wayne Stehbens, who produces excellent wines across the board. This one offers flavours that are complex and layered, with depth and breadth. It has a soft, attractive texture, and is dry with a light-to-medium tannic grip. It's excellent with any dish featuring red meat.

NOTES

....

....

....

....

★ ★ ★ ½

Lindemans 'Bin 40' Merlot 2007

SOUTH EASTERN AUSTRALIA $12.95   (458679)

Bin 40? So have I, and I'm as youthful and vibrant as this Merlot! Merlot is the second most planted grape variety in the world. There's a lot of it around, some of it mediocre, but Bin 40 is a cut above. It has good, solid fruit and a firm, tangy texture, and it's dry and medium bodied with light tannins. It goes very nicely with well-seasoned, grilled red meats.

NOTES

....

....

....

....

★ ★ ★

Lindemans 'Bin 45' Cabernet Sauvignon 2007

SOUTH EASTERN AUSTRALIA $12.95   (119628)

Dr. Lindeman was a doctor in 19th-century Australia, a winemaker and a supporter of the temperance movement because he thought moderate wine-drinking was good for one's health. He'd be pleased with modern Lindemans, I expect. This Cabernet Sauvignon has plenty of intense fruit flavour and a juicy texture that seems to invite food along for the ride. Drink it with red meats or with rich pork dishes.

NOTES

....

....

....

....

Lindemans 'Bin 50' Shiraz 2007

★ ★ ★ ½

SOUTH EASTERN AUSTRALIA $12.95   (145367)

There are countless Australian Shirazes out there. How are we to distinguish among them? For me, the critical characteristic is balance. Many Shirazes are packed with flavour, but they're too heavy and dense for food. Others, like this one, achieve excellent balance among fruit, acid and tannins. Dry and medium-bodied, it's good with roast chicken or a grilled veal chop.

NOTES

....

....

....

....

Lindemans 'Bin 99' Pinot Noir 2007

★ ★ ★ ½

SOUTH EASTERN AUSTRALIA $14.00   (458661)

Pinot Noir made big strides in popularity in North America after it featured in the movie *Sideways*, but it isn't so big on the Australian wine scene. Even so, this is a pretty nice entry-level Pinot that offers ripe fruit flavours. It's medium bodied and dry, and it's a wine for all seasons and seasonings; serve it on the patio with grilled lamb or with hearty winter dishes like lamb stew.

NOTES

....

....

....

....

Little Penguin Merlot 2007

★ ★ ★

SOUTH EASTERN AUSTRALIA $12.15   (598912)

Little penguins (as distinct from the bigger kind you see in Antarctica) are found along some of Australia's southern coasts. This bird has swum a long way to bring several varieties of wine. The Merlot is straightforward and well made. It offers quite concentrated flavours and a rich and tangy texture. Fruit-forward and mouth-filling, it goes well with spicy food like barbecued beef and ribs.

NOTES

....

....

....

★ ★ ★ ★

Long Flat Cabernet/Merlot 2006

SOUTH EASTERN AUSTRALIA $12.85 (24802)

[1-Litre Tetra Pak] This works out to about $10 per standard 750 mL wine bottle, which is a pretty good buy. For that price you get a well-made red blend that delivers solid flavours of ripe fruit. It's dry and medium bodied, and it has a tangy, spicy texture that lightens the fruitiness. It goes nicely with a range of red meat dishes. Try it with grilled steak or with a red meat stew.

NOTES

★ ★ ★ ★

McWilliam's 'Hanwood Estate' Shiraz 2006

SOUTH EASTERN AUSTRALIA $14.45 (610683)

Many Australian Shirazes in this price range taste very similar, so it's nice to come across one with some individuality. This has the layered ripe fruit flavours of a well-made Shiraz and some light oakiness from the barrels in which it was aged. It's medium bodied and has a slightly tangy texture. It goes well with grilled lamb chops or with a pepper steak.

NOTES

★ ★ ★

McWilliam's 'J. J. McWilliam' Shiraz/Cabernet 2006

SOUTH EASTERN AUSTRALIA $10.15 (16701)

Australians have put this blend on the map, whether it's Shiraz or Cabernet that's the dominant component. This one delivers tangy flavours and an equally zesty, fairly light texture, and it's an excellent wine choice when you're serving grilled red meats or even lighter dishes such as meatloaf, pizza, or rotisserie chicken. It's just medium bodied and dry, with minimal tannins.

NOTES

Palandri Cabernet Sauvignon 2003

★ ★ ★ ★ ½   WESTERN AUSTRALIA $16.85   (23614)

So many great wines come out of Western Australia. Here's one of them.
This Cabernet is big and full of rich fruit flavours with plenty of complexity.
It's dry, with very firm tannins, and you can even tuck this away for a year
or two. But if you plan to drink it soon, have some rare to medium-rare red
meat on hand to neutralize the tannins and bring out the wine's fruitiness.

NOTES
....
....
....
....
....

Penfolds 'Koonunga Hill' Cabernet Sauvignon 2006

★ ★ ★ ★ ½   SOUTH AUSTRALIA $16.40   (45625)

Penfolds is one of the great names in Australian winemaking, not least
because it produces Grange, the country's most sought-after wine. The
Koonunga Hill range is dirt cheap in comparison, but they're all good
quality. This is a beautiful Cabernet that has concentrated but finely
nuanced flavours and an intense, tangy texture. It's very dry, with gripping
tannins, so drink it with red meat cooked no more than medium-rare.

NOTES
....
....
....
....

Penfolds 'Koonunga Hill' Shiraz 2005

★ ★ ★ ★ ½   SOUTH EASTERN AUSTRALIA $16.95   (642751)

Penfolds's top wine, Grange, is close to 100 percent Shiraz. At hundreds
of dollars a bottle, it's a rare treat, but if you're looking for a less expensive
Shiraz that delivers real quality, try this one from the same stable. It's
fruit-forward—rich and sweet with ripe fruit, with a big, intense, and
tangy texture. Dry and medium-bodied, it's a great choice if you're having
grilled or roast lamb. If not, any well-seasoned red meat goes nicely with it.

NOTES
....
....
....

Penfolds 'Koonunga Hill' Shiraz/Cabernet 2006

★ ★ ★ ★

SOUTH EASTERN AUSTRALIA $16.35   (285544)

Penfolds is so committed to its wines that it regularly sends winemaker
Peter Gago around the world to hold re-corking clinics where owners of
older vintages of Penfolds wines can have the corks replaced. No need for
that yet with this lovely blend. It delivers rich and layered flavours, very
good and complex structure, and a stylish, tangy texture. It's moderately
tannic, so drink it with medium-rare red meat or aged cheddar.

NOTES

....

....

....

....

Penfolds 'Thomas Hyland' Shiraz 2005

★ ★ ★ ★ ½

SOUTH AUSTRALIA $19.80   (611210)

[Vintages Essential] This big, luscious Shiraz is named for the son-in-law
of Dr. Penfold, who founded the company. Thomas would be delighted
to be associated with it. It's an assertive red with intense fruit flavours and
has a texture that's plush, dense, and tangy. Medium- to full-bodied, it's
a sheer pleasure to drink—especially with well-seasoned red meat, like
lamb with garlic and rosemary.

NOTES

....

....

....

....

Penmara Wines 'The Five Families' Shiraz 2006

★ ★ ★ ★

NEW SOUTH WALES $14.15   (565929)

This wine is a collaborative effort by five wineries, and the name combines
pen, from the Greek prefix for "five," with *mara*, the Aboriginal word for
"five fingers." Their dry, medium-bodied Shiraz is very well made, with
concentrated and focused fruit flavours. The texture is lively and fresh,
making this an excellent wine for turkey and cranberries as much as for
red meats.

NOTES

....

....

....

....

Peter Lehmann 'Clancy's Legendary Red' 2005

★ ★ ★ ★ ½

BAROSSA VALLEY $18.80 (611467)

Clancy is just about a household name in Australia, where it has won many awards. It's a delicious blend of Shiraz, Cabernet Sauvignon, and Merlot and delivers terrific depth and breadth of flavour, enhanced by plenty of complexity. Full-bodied with a dense and tangy texture, it's dry and carries its tannins lightly. You can't go wrong pouring this with hearty red meat dishes.

NOTES

Peter Lehmann Shiraz 2005

★ ★ ★ ★

BAROSSA VALLEY $19.90 (572875)

Peter Lehmann is one of the icons of the Australian wine industry, and his big, bold presence is reflected in some of his wines. Like this one. It's a classic Barossa Shiraz that's dry, with full, ripe fruit flavours, nice complexity, and a stylish, tangy texture. It has high alcohol (14.5 percent) but it's well managed and doesn't intrude into the flavours or texture. This is a perfect match for barbecued red meats.

NOTES

Peter Lehmann Shiraz/Grenache 2007

★ ★ ★ ★ ½

BAROSSA VALLEY $15.95 (610725)

Peter Lehmann's take on the Shiraz-Grenache blend produces a marvellously complex and broad-flavoured red with a lovely tangy and juicy texture. It's medium bodied, dry with light tannins, and leaves its flavours in your mouth for some time. This is definitely a wine that calls for food and, given where it's from, lamb springs to mind. Pair it with seasoned (rosemary, garlic) lamb chops, grilled medium-rare.

NOTES

Red Knot Shiraz 2006

★ ★ ★ ★ ½

MCLAREN VALE $17.15   (619395)

This wine sports one of the more unusual closures. First you unwind its plastic tail, then the whole thing comes off. After playing with that, you get to taste the wine, which is a bigger treat. It's plush and densely flavoured and has a generous and smooth texture. There's some tanginess there, too, but in general it's balanced away from acidity. This goes nicely with well-seasoned red meats like barbecued ribs.

NOTES

....

....

....

....

Rosemount 'Diamond Label' Cabernet/Merlot 2006

★ ★ ★ ½

SOUTH EASTERN AUSTRALIA $14.00   (552000)

This Cabernet/Merlot is just the thing for mid-week (or weekend) barbecues. Toss some pieces of well-marinated red meat onto the grill and pull the cork on the bottle. The flavours are concentrated and quite rich, and the texture is tangy and very nicely balanced. It's dry and medium bodied, a very successful accompaniment to a hearty red-meat winter stew.

NOTES

....

....

....

....

....

Rosemount 'Diamond Label' Cabernet Sauvignon 2005

★ ★ ★ ★

SOUTH EASTERN AUSTRALIA $17.00   (334870)

Rosemount's "Diamond Label" wines are extremely reliable across the board. This Cabernet Sauvignon is well made, with solid fruit flavours and a mouth-filling and tangy texture. The tannins are perceptible, but they're light and easy. It's medium bodied and dry and goes well with a wide range of food, especially red meat—burgers, grilled lamb, or steak.

NOTES

....

....

....

....

....

Rosemount Estate 'Diamond Label' Merlot 2006

★ ★ ★ ½

SOUTH EASTERN AUSTRALIA $17.00   (542431)

There's a sense out there that Merlot is a sort of red Chardonnay. It's the most popular red (just as Chardonnay's the number one white), and it's often made to be easy drinking and, well, fairly boring. But this Merlot isn't any of that. It has quite intense flavours and a very solid and tangy texture. It's medium bodied and dry, with light tannins, and is a good choice for roast chicken or turkey, or a grilled veal chop.

NOTES

Rosemount Estate 'Diamond Label' Shiraz 2006

★ ★ ★ ★

SOUTH EASTERN AUSTRALIA $17.00   (302349)

This is almost a classic Australian Shiraz. It's been in LCBO stores for many, many years, and I'm pleased with the evolution of the style. It's all there, the rich, ripe flavours and the tangy texture that you expect. But it's not overbearing, not in your face. It's medium bodied with a dry, lightly tangy texture, has good structure, and is excellent with grilled lamb chops or roast lamb.

NOTES

Rosemount Estate 'Diamond Label' Shiraz/Cabernet 2007

★ ★ ★ ½

SOUTH EASTERN AUSTRALIA $14.05   (214270)

Like the other wines in Rosemount's "Diamond Label" series, the Shiraz/Cabernet is from the huge South Eastern Australia wine zone, which covers the bulk of Australia's wine regions. It allows producers to source their grapes from many different areas. This blend offers solid flavours that are ripe and concentrated and a mid-weight texture that's fruity and very lightly tannic. Open a bottle of this when you're serving hamburgers.

NOTES

Silver Leaf Cabernet Merlot 2006

★ ★ ★

SOUTH EASTERN AUSTRALIA $14.85   (64865)

[1-Litre PET Bottle] PET is a food-grade plastic that does not taint the wine and, because it's much lighter than glass, demands less fuel for shipping. The wine inside is a no-nonsense blend that delivers good, straightforward flavours and a solid, tangy texture. It's medium bodied and dry and goes well with a range of foods: roast chicken, pizza, burgers, and simply prepared red meat dishes.

NOTES

....

....

....

....

Wolf Blass 'Grey Label' Cabernet Sauvignon 2005

★ ★ ★ ★ ★

LANGHORNE CREEK $36.00   (470120)

These charcoal grey labels look both elegant and authoritative, and they represent the wine very effectively. Like the Shiraz in the next review, this Cabernet is dense and powerful in flavour and texture, but none of this is at the expense of style, structure, or the variety. This is as much a Cabernet as the "Grey Label" Shiraz is all Shiraz. Open this as you toss a fine cut of beef on the barbecue.

NOTES

....

....

....

....

Wolf Blass 'Grey Label' Shiraz 2005

★ ★ ★ ★ ★

MCLAREN VALE $36.00   (390872)

Oh, my, God! Here's the essence of Australian Shiraz, the sort of wine Aussie Shiraz–lovers dream about. This vintage is from McLaren Vale. (The region varies each year, depending on the quality of the grapes.) The Grey Wolf delivers fruit-driven power at the flavour end of things and a gorgeous mouth-filling texture. Dry and medium- to full-bodied, it's a great wine for grilled red meats.

NOTES

....

....

....

....

AUSTRALIA | THE REDS

Wolf Blass 'Premium Selection' Cabernet Sauvignon 2005

★★★★ ½

SOUTH AUSTRALIA $24.75   (321927)

[Vintages Essential] Cabernet Sauvignon ought to have pretty intense flavours, good structure, and pleasant tannins, whether they're young and gripping or evolved and more integrated. This Cab meets all the requirements and more. You'll find the flavours rich, complex, and structured, the texture full and balanced, and the tannins prominent but manageable with rare or medium-rare red meats or aged cheeses.

NOTES

Wolf Blass 'Premium Selection' Shiraz 2005

★★★★ ½

SOUTH AUSTRALIA $25.95   (348540)

[Vintages Essential] The complexity in this dry Shiraz earns it a rating higher than many others. You'll find all the sweet and intense flavours you expect, together with a generous and fairly tangy texture. But it's well structured and nicely nuanced. It's a bit more than medium bodied and reasonably high (15 percent) in alcohol, although you wouldn't know it from the taste. It's an obvious candidate for grilled red meats.

NOTES

Wolf Blass 'Red Label' Shiraz/Cabernet Sauvignon 2006

★★★ ½

SOUTH EASTERN AUSTRALIA $14.85   (311795)

Wolf Blass got the idea of colour-coding his wine labels from horse racing: Spectators tracked their horses around the course by the colours the jockeys were wearing. This Shiraz/Cabernet Sauvignon from the Blass stable is a well-made, straightforward blend that delivers solid and complex fruit. It's medium bodied, smooth textured, and a great match for lamb shanks.

NOTES

Wolf Blass 'Red Label' Shiraz/Grenache 2006

★ ★ ★ ★

SOUTH EASTERN AUSTRALIA $14.95   (494336)

Shiraz and Grenache (both varieties common in southern France) make compelling blends, and this is no exception. It's rich in layers of flavour that sweep into your mouth on a tangy tide. There's some fruit sweetness from the Grenache, but this is a dry red, medium bodied, with light tannins. It's an excellent choice when you're serving red meats or hearty stews.

NOTES

....
....
....
....
....

Wolf Blass 'Yellow Label' Cabernet Sauvignon 2006

★ ★ ★ ★

SOUTH AUSTRALIA $17.95   (251876)

There was a time when no self-respecting restaurant would leave this off its wine list. It was everyone's standby for steak, red meat in general, and in fact for any food. Taste it and you'll see the attraction. It's just well made and delivers above par in flavour, texture, and finish. You'll find intense fruitiness and a full and tangy mouth feel in this dry, medium-bodied Cab.

NOTES

....
....
....

Wolf Blass 'Yellow Label' Pinot Noir 2007

★ ★ ★ ★

VICTORIA $17.80   (611509)

Many of Victoria's grape-growing regions are cool-climate, making them suitable for Pinot Noir. This one is well made, with flavours that are quite concentrated and complex. The texture is tangy and crisp, and the balance is weighted towards food. Dry and medium-bodied, this is a good choice when you're grilling Atlantic salmon, veal, or lamb chops.

NOTES

....
....
....
....

Wyndham Estate 'Bin 555' Shiraz 2005

★ ★ ★ ★

SOUTH EASTERN AUSTRALIA $16.25   (189415)

Founded in 1828, Wyndham Estate is Australia's oldest operating winery. George Wyndham, an English immigrant, planted the first commercial Shiraz vineyard. He had no idea what he'd started. This Shiraz, harvested in the winery's 180th year, delivers plush fruit flavours and a generous, mouth-filling, and refreshing texture. It's an obvious choice for roast or grilled lamb.

NOTES
....
....
....
....

Yalumba 'Y Series' Shiraz/Viognier 2006

★ ★ ★ ★

SOUTH AUSTRALIA $14.15   (624494)

The inspiration to add Viognier, a white grape, to Shiraz comes from the northern Rhône Valley in France, where producers have long added a little Viognier to give the aromas and flavours of their Syrahs (Shirazes) a lift. It sure works here. Both aromas and flavours are lovely and complex, and the texture is rich and tangy. Medium-bodied and dry, this is an excellent choice for grilled lamb chops.

NOTES
....
....
....
....

Yellow Tail Merlot 2007

★ ★ ★

SOUTH EASTERN AUSTRALIA $12.20   (625350)

Yellow Tail is the wine success story of the decade. It has all the elements of drama: the little family winery that thought big, though probably had no idea *how* big, big would be. This Merlot is, too. It's full and brash in flavour and texture, although it's very modest in terms of complexity. But if you're looking for a fruit-forward red that will please many people at a barbecue, this might be it. Serve it with juicy hamburgers.

NOTES
....
....
....
....

BRITISH COLUMBIA

BRITISH COLUMBIA'S WINERIES—most them located in the Okanagan Valley—produce a lot of high-quality and well-priced red wine. Unfortunately, hardly any of it makes its way to Ontario because nearly all the wine made in British Columbia is consumed there.

The VQA classification on British Columbia wine labels means that the grapes were grown in the region specified and that the wine has been tested and tasted to ensure quality.

Mission Hill Reserve Cabernet Sauvignon 2006

★ ★ ★ ★ ½   VQA OKANAGAN VALLEY $24.95   (553321)

[Vintages Essential] Mission Hill helped put the Okanagan Valley wine region on the map, and the company's attention to detail has kept it in the forefront of British Columbia wine producers. This Reserve Cabernet Sauvignon is stylish and opulent. You'll find elegant fruit flavours and a rich and tangy texture. Dry and a bit more than medium-bodied, it goes nicely with well-seasoned red meats.

NOTES

....

....

....

....

....

BULGARIA

BULGARIA PRODUCES A LOT OF WINE, but it's poorly represented on LCBO shelves. The country's wine industry is still finding its feet after the end of the communist era, when Bulgaria churned out huge volumes of mediocre wine for Eastern Europe. The good news is that there are many quality wines (Cabernet Sauvignon and Merlot among them) made in Bulgaria. When they find their way to Ontario, they'll add to the range of values in the LCBO.

Domaine Boyar Cabernet Sauvignon 2006

★ ★ ★

THRACIAN VALLEY $7.85   (340851)

Domaine Boyar is one of Bulgaria's biggest wine producers, and this Cabernet Sauvignon has been available in the LCBO for years. It's a straightforward red with some Cabernet character in the fruit flavours and a mid-weight tangy texture. At this price, it's a good buy for parties and get-togethers, and it goes well with burgers and pizzas as well as with red meats.

NOTES

....

....

....

....

....

CALIFORNIA

CALIFORNIA'S WINE INDUSTRY began in earnest in the 1850s, soon after the Gold Rush had subsided. It fell on hard times during Prohibition in the 1920s and early 1930s, but was given a boost when, in 1976, California wines beat some of the best Bordeaux in a blind-tasting in Paris. California now accounts for 90 percent of the wine produced in the United States, and is fourth in world production after France, Italy and Spain.

California's varied growing conditions are suitable for many different grape varieties and wine styles. The state's signature grape is Zinfandel (the excuse for many zin-fully bad puns), but Cabernet Sauvignon is more important. Other significant varieties are Merlot, Shiraz/Syrah, and Pinot Noir.

Most of the value wines in this book are labelled "California," which means that producers can use grapes grown anywhere in the state. Important designated regions within the state include Napa Valley, Sonoma County, Mendocino, and Paso Robles.

★ ★ ★ ★
Beaulieu Vineyard 'BV Coastal Estates' Cabernet Sauvignon 2005

CALIFORNIA $13.05   (569871)

The flavours of this Cabernet Sauvignon are rich and ripe, layered and complex. They're accompanied by a round and generous texture with a little acid bite making for a tangy feel. Dry and medium-bodied, with moderate tannins, it's ideal for a wide range of foods, including red meats, hearty vegetarian stews, and pasta in a rich tomato and meat sauce.

NOTES
....
....
....
....

★ ★ ★ ★ ★
Beringer Cabernet Sauvignon 2005

KNIGHTS VALLEY $39.95   (352583)

[Vintages Essential] This is a stunning wine, vintage after vintage. It achieves the feat that distinguishes many fine wines, of being both bold and stylish at the same time. The flavours are deep, broad, and intricately layered, the texture is plump, plush, and generous, and the acidity is beautifully handled. The tannins are still gripping, so you might decant it two or three hours before enjoying it with beef, grilled or roasted no more than medium-rare.

NOTES
....
....
....
....

★ ★ ★ ★
Beringer 'Founders' Estate' Cabernet Sauvignon 2005

CALIFORNIA $19.95   (534263)

Beringer is the Napa Valley's oldest continuous wine producer, dating back to 1876. It stayed in business even during the dry days of Prohibition by making sacramental wine. This Cabernet is delicious rather than spiritual, and delivers a medium body, intense and juicy texture, and good solid fruit flavours. It's dry, the tannins are moderate, and it goes very well with steak.

NOTES
....
....
....
....

Beringer 'Stone Cellars' Cabernet Sauvignon 2006

★ ★ ★ ½

CALIFORNIA $14.00   (606798)

In the 1870s, the cliffs at the Beringer winery in the Napa Valley were excavated to form extensive cellars for aging the wine away from the California heat. Now mostly a museum, the almost 150-year-old vaults are celebrated in this "Stone Cellars" line. The Cabernet does them proud, with its concentrated, fresh flavours, tangy texture, and drying tannins. It's quite a lovely Cab that you'll enjoy with lamb or beef.

NOTES

....

....

....

....

Black Anvil Shiraz 2005

★ ★ ★

CALIFORNIA $12.70   (45567)

You can often ignore descriptions on wine labels, but sometimes they get it right. This one reads, "The ultimate barbecue wine. Big bold flavours. Great with burgers." Well, maybe it's not the ultimate, but it sure goes well with grilled meat. It has rich, intense flavours and a smooth texture that's light on tannins. It's medium bodied, fruity, and easy drinking.

NOTES

....

....

....

....

....

Black Box Cabernet Sauvignon 2006

★ ★ ★ ★

PASO ROBLES $13.95   (38331)

[1-Litre Tetra Pak] Paso Robles became a hot wine region (in terms of popularity) a few years ago, when many stellar wines began to emerge from it. Black Box shows that they can do it in a popular style, too. This Cab is quite classy, with layered, complex fruit flavours, and a refreshing and juicy texture. It's medium weight and dry, with easygoing tannins, and in its soft package, it's a natural for barbecues on the deck or for picnics.

NOTES

....

....

....

★ ★ ★ ★ ½ **Bonterra Vineyards Cabernet Sauvignon 2006**
MENDOCINO COUNTY $19.95   (342428)

[Vintages Essential] Bonterra wines are organic: The grapes are grown organically, the wine is made organically, and the winery is maintained without the use of artificial chemicals. This a beautiful Cabernet Sauvignon that delivers ripe, concentrated flavours and a plush and tangy texture that fills your mouth. The tannins are quite firm, so drink it with red meats cooked medium-rare at most.

NOTES
....
....
....
....

★ ★ ★ ★ ★ **Cline Syrah 2006**
SONOMA VALLEY $12.95   (733758)

[Vintages Essential] The Sonoma Valley lies next to the better-known Napa Valley. In contrast to the busy, commercialized Napa, Sonoma seems restfully rural. But there's nothing sleepy about the wines, as this classic Sonoma Syrah shows. It has dynamic, rich flavour, a medium-to-full body, refreshing texture, and good tannic structure. It's great with grilled lamb or steak.

NOTES
....
....
....
....

★ ★ ★ ★ **Cline Zinfandel 2006**
CALIFORNIA $12.90   (489278)

This is a good example of a Zinfandel made to go with a meal—unlike too many high-octane, high-performance Zins that leave food in the dust. This one has a refreshing texture (not a heavy, low-acid one), and the concentrated ripe flavours are layered. It's medium bodied and the very dry texture works well with its fruitiness. This is a natural for juicy hamburgers or other well-seasoned red meats.

NOTES
....
....
....
....

Dancing Bull Cabernet Sauvignon 2005

★ ★ ★

CALIFORNIA $11.95   (30023)

The bull on the bottle looks pretty happy. Maybe he's been into the wine?
It's a straightforward, uncomplicated Cabernet with sweet fruit at its core.
It's dry with light tannins, a medium body, and a good fruity texture. It
goes well with tasty hamburgers and spicy red meats. No bull, except on
the label.

NOTES

Dancing Bull Zinfandel 2006

★ ★ ★ ★

CALIFORNIA $11.95   (669499)

This is a food-friendly kind of Zinfandel, unlike so many that are full of
jammy fruit, with over-the-top alcohol, and a sticky, viscous texture. I
mean, they have their place, too, but it's rarely at the table. The happy bull
has choreographed a Zin that's full of ripe fruit, but it stresses flavour over
sheer power. And the texture, although substantial, is fresh and light. This
is a Zin you can happily pair with ribs or steak slathered in barbecue sauce.

NOTES

Dog House 'Maxie's Merlot' 2004

★ ★ ★

CALIFORNIA $13.95   (614156)

Dog House is from California's Kendall-Jackson winery, which could
have renamed itself Kennel-Jackson. With this pedigree behind her,
Maxie has made a Merlot that's a cut above many of the animal brands
that litter LCBO shelves. Look for nicely structured ripe, dark fruit flavours, moderate tannins, and a good tangy texture. Don't "kibble" about
a food match: Lap this up with a plate of red meat.

NOTES

Fetzer 'Valley Oaks' Cabernet Sauvignon 2005

★★★ ½

CALIFORNIA $15.00 (336974)

Fetzer cultivates its vineyards in a sustainable way by avoiding artificial pesticides and other chemical treatments. This Cabernet has solid, even intense, flavours, with a very attractive tanginess to the texture. It's medium bodied and dry, with easygoing tannins. It teams well with traditional roast beef and vegetables but partners just as successfully with a hearty portobello burger.

NOTES

....

....

....

....

Fetzer 'Valley Oaks' Zinfandel 2006

★★★★

CALIFORNIA $15.00 (234617)

Fetzer wines are made from grapes grown using sustainable agricultural methods. This Zinfandel is packed with flavour, as you'd expect from the variety, but it's not over the top, or sweet. With an attractive tangy texture, it's medium bodied and dry, and you'll find it goes well with spicy meat or vegetarian dishes.

NOTES

....

....

....

....

Fish Eye Shiraz 2005

★★★ ½

CALIFORNIA $10.00 (035113)

Although Australia dominates the Shiraz market, there are good-to-excellent Shirazes from other regions, too, including California. This wine offers quite concentrated sweet and spicy fruit flavours. It's medium bodied, has a texture that's tangy, and goes well with grilled spicy sausages and pizzas that have sweet toppings like mango or red peppers.

NOTES

....

....

....

....

Fox Brook Cabernet Sauvignon 2005
★ ★ ★
CALIFORNIA $9.15 (620781)

One of the complaints often made about wines made from native American grapes is that they tasted "foxy." No one knows why this characteristic is called that, but the good thing is that there's none of it in this Cabernet. What you get is a straightforward, medium-bodied, dry red that has good, upfront fruit flavours, and a smooth and plump texture. It's ideal for a crowd (or a couple) dining on hamburgers.

NOTES

Gallo Family Vineyards Cabernet Sauvignon 2006
★ ★ ★ ★
SONOMA COUNTY $17.00 (354274)

Gallo is based in Sonoma, so this is from the heartland. A quite stylish Cabernet, with layered and complex flavours, it's medium bodied and dry, and is restrained through and through, rather than having the fruit-forward style you often think of as Californian. The texture is refreshing and tangy, and this is a very successful choice if you're serving grilled or roasted red meats or game.

NOTES

Gallo 'Turning Leaf' Reserve Cabernet Sauvignon 2005
★ ★ ★
CALIFORNIA $12.45 (412296)

Gallo's "Turning Leaf" line offers good value across the board. This dry, medium-bodied Cabernet Sauvignon delivers straightforward flavours and a solid texture with light tannic astringency. Falling leaves make you think of the transition from summer to winter, but this is an all-season wine, as good with barbecued meats as with hearty winter stews.

NOTES

Gnarly Head 'Cab' Cabernet Sauvignon 2005

★ ★ ★ ½

CALIFORNIA $16.95   (68924)

The label shows a stylized and very gnarly grapevine, making you think this could be from old vines. There's no such claim, but the wine has the flavour concentration you often associate with older vines. Look for intense, sweet fruit flavours here, with a generous texture and drying tannins. It's medium-to-full in weight, and goes with heavier food, such as steak.

NOTES

....

....

....

....

....

Leaping Horse Merlot 2005

★ ★ ★ ½

CALIFORNIA $12.25   (613265)

Horses aren't as common as other animals on wine labels. But don't be a neigh-sayer or look this one in the mouth. Trot down to the LCBO and get a bottle. This attractive, dry Merlot is medium bodied and delivers solid flavours. The texture is quite lean, and the tannins are drying. Drink it with a grilled veal chop or with juicy hamburgers.

NOTES

....

....

....

....

....

Liberty School Cabernet Sauvignon 2006

★ ★ ★ ★ ★

CALIFORNIA $16.95   (738823)

[Vintages Essential] Skylar Stuck, export manager of Treana Winery, which makes Liberty School, describes this as "a step and a half above any other Cab we've made." This is one of the great buys in the LCBO. It over-delivers on everything, with compelling, concentrated, ripe aromas and flavours, a generous, mouth-filling, and tangy texture, sweet tannins, and a long finish. It's a natural for rich red meat dishes.

NOTES

....

....

....

....

Napa Valley Vineyards Reserve Cabernet Sauvignon 2005
★ ★ ★ ★   NAPA VALLEY $18.00   (29975)

Napa Valley and Cabernet Sauvignon have become successful partners in wine, and for good reason. The valley not only provides excellent growing conditions, but Napa winemakers have developed their skills so that they seldom go wrong. Here's an example of that expertise in a well-made and complex Cabernet that delivers in both flavour and texture. Dry and moderately tannic, it's a natural for steak.

NOTES

Napa Valley Vineyards Reserve Merlot 2003
★ ★ ★ ★ ½   NAPA VALLEY $18.00   (29983)

Napa Valley Vineyards sells this wine in a robust bottle, which gives it the appearance and feel of substance. And it is a substantial wine, not in the sense of being heavy and weighty, but in quality. The flavours are concentrated and full but complex, and the texture is tangy but also refreshing. It's dry and medium weight, with moderate tannins, and goes well with simply prepared red meats.

NOTES

Ravenswood 'Vintners Blend' Zinfandel 2006
★ ★ ★ ★   CALIFORNIA $17.95   (359257)

[Vintages Essential] In many ways, this is a classic California Zinfandel, with plush, in-your-face ripe fruit. But it also has a sort of elegance you don't always find in high-octane Zinfandels. This one is full flavoured, to be sure, but it's light on its feet and has a clean, fresh texture that makes it especially good for food. Open this summer or winter when you're serving grilled red meats.

NOTES

★ ★ ★ ★ **R.H. Phillips 'Night Harvest' Shiraz 2005**

CALIFORNIA $13.95   (576272)

Unfortunately no relation to this book's author, R.H. Phillips is located a short drive north of San Francisco. "Night Harvest" refers to picking the grapes after dark, when the cool air keeps them fresh and preserves their acidity. The result here is a finely made, stylish Shiraz that's complex and well balanced, dry with a medium body. It goes nicely with well-seasoned roasted and grilled red meat dishes.

NOTES
....
....
....
....

★ ★ ★ ★ ★ **Robert Mondavi Cabernet Sauvignon 2005**

NAPA VALLEY $37.95   (255513)

[Vintages Essential] How much should you pay for a Napa Cab? Only the fare shown on the meter. The tariff here is a bit higher than you usually find in the LCBO, but—wow!—this is a delicious Cabernet. It's elegant and stylish right through, with delicious and complex flavours. It's dry and medium bodied, with moderate tannins and a sleek and quite refreshing texture. Serve it with rack of lamb.

NOTES
....
....
....
....

★ ★ ★ ★ **Robert Mondavi 'Private Selection' Merlot 2005**

CALIFORNIA $18.95   (524769)

If you're having a dinner party featuring grilled lamb or other red meat and you want an attractive, stylish red, give this Merlot a go. It has complex, ripe fruit flavours and a generous and slightly tangy texture. It's dry and the tannins are definitely present, but serving the meat on the rare side will cut through them and bring out the fruit.

NOTES
....
....
....
....
....

Robert Mondavi 'Private Selection' Pinot Noir 2006

★ ★ ★ ★

CENTRAL COAST $18.95   (465435)

This Pinot Noir has a deceptively light colour. You might expect a wimpy, thin Pinot, but what you actually get are quite intense flavours of fresh, ripe fruit. Medium-bodied and dry, with a smooth, easy-drinking texture and light tannins, this is a real pleasure to pour, and lives up to the quality associated with the Mondavi name. Pair it with grilled planked salmon.

NOTES

....

....

....

....

....

Rosenblum Zinfandel 2005

★ ★ ★ ★

CALIFORNIA $17.95   (284653)

[Vintages Essential] The three wineries most often associated with Zinfandel start with the letter R—Ravenswood, Ridge, and this one, Rosenblum. Each has its fans, and you might well become one after you taste this. It has all the usual Zinfandel character—rich, intense fruit, a plush and fleshy texture, and high alcohol. But it's well balanced and can be drunk with spicy red meat dishes.

NOTES

....

....

....

....

Smoking Loon Cabernet Sauvignon 2006

★ ★ ★ ½

CALIFORNIA $17.95   (55517)

Why is this loon smoking? Because this is a smokin' Cabernet? It's chock full of rich fruit flavours and has an attractive texture that's quite mouth filling but still refreshing and good for food. Drink this with grilled red meats at the cottage while you're listening for the loons. Don't hear them? It's because they've taken up smoking and can't call with cigars in their beaks.

NOTES

....

....

....

....

Sonoma Vineyards Merlot 2004

★ ★ ★ ★ ½

SONOMA COUNTY $19.45   (60632)

Sonoma County often lies in the shadow of its better-known and more tourist-overrun neighbour, Napa. But great wines come from Sonoma, too, as this terrific Merlot shows. The fruit flavours here are concentrated, pure, and delicious. The texture is smooth and juicy, and the balance excellent. Dry and medium-bodied and a real treat to drink, it does very well with grilled red meats and even herbed roast chicken.

NOTES

....

....

....

....

Sterling Vineyards Cabernet Sauvignon 2005

★ ★ ★ ★ ★

NAPA VALLEY $29.70   (314575)

[Vintages Essential] No wonder Napa and Cab go so effortlessly together. Wines like this make you appreciate how growing conditions and wine-making experience can combine to achieve excellence. This classy Cab delivers beautifully nuanced flavours that roll in like waves, and they mesh seamlessly with its finely balanced and silky texture. There's good tannin in this dry and medium-bodied Cab, so drink it with rare to medium-rare red meat.

NOTES

....

....

....

Sterling Vineyards Merlot 2004

★ ★ ★ ★ ½

NAPA VALLEY $29.70   (330241)

[Vintages Essential] There are two dominant styles of New World Merlot: dull, generic, and lacking much structure, or intense, complex, and well structured. This is one of the latter. It's delicious and delivers rich and complex flavours that ride harmoniously on a sleek texture. It's dry and medium- to full-bodied, and has quite firm tannins. This is red wine for red meat.

NOTES

....

....

....

....

Sterling Vineyards 'Vintner's Collection' Merlot 2005

★ ★ ★ ½

CENTRAL COAST $15.95   (622837)

Sterling is one of California's premier wineries, producing quality across its portfolio. This Merlot is in an easy-drinking style, with fairly plush fruit and a smooth, mouth-filling texture. It's medium bodied and dry with tannins you can feel, and it makes an excellent choice for well-seasoned or spicy red meat dishes. Try it with barbecued ribs or peppery kebabs.

NOTES
....
....
....
....
....

Sutter Home Merlot 2006

★ ★ ★

CALIFORNIA $10.95   (344549)

The California Gold Rush started with the discovery of gold at Sutter's Mill, as the name of this winery reminds us. A Grape Rush followed and saw the birth of the California wine industry. This is a medium-bodied, juicy textured Merlot that delivers a core of sweet fruit flavour. Not overly complex, it makes a good partner for mid-week burgers or grilled red meat.

NOTES
....
....
....
....
....

Three Thieves 'Bandit' Cabernet Sauvignon 2004

★ ★ ★

CALIFORNIA $12.95   (622001)

[1-Litre Tetra Pak] If some people still have reservations about wine in a Tetra Pak, they're not likely to be won over by boxes that look like this. It's too bad because there are some good wines in boxes waiting to be discovered. This Cabernet is bold and fruity, with a tangy texture. It's dry, straightforward and uncomplicated, and goes well with spicy barbecue-style food, especially herbed sausages.

NOTES
....
....
....
....

Twin Fin Shiraz 2005

★ ★ ★ ★

CALIFORNIA $12.95   (34132)

This is like essence of New World red. It's all pure, sweet, ripe fruit that's upfront, intense, and mouth coating. Medium-bodied and in a dry, lightly tannic style, it has a smooth, generous, and mouth-filling texture. With a label featuring a classic convertible and a surfboard, it's aimed at baby boomers. Crank up the Beach Boys and the barbecue, and toss on a steak. Older and younger people can play along, too.

NOTES

....

....

....

....

Wente 'Southern Hills' Cabernet Sauvignon 2005

★ ★ ★ ★ ½

LIVERMORE VALLEY/SAN FRANCISCO BAY $17.05   (301507)

These regions near San Francisco were first planted with vines by Spanish missionaries in the 1760s. The Wente family arrived a little later, in the 1840s. Powerful, intense, and full of layers of rich fruit flavour, this full-bodied Cabernet delivers a texture that's tangy and refreshing. The tannins are moderate, and you can tame them a little by drinking this with red meat grilled or roasted no more than medium-rare.

NOTES

....

....

....

....

Woodbridge Cabernet Sauvignon 2006

★ ★ ★

CALIFORNIA $13.45   (48611)

This strikes me as the best of the Woodbridge reds in the LCBO (the others are a Zinfandel and a Merlot). Woodbridge is a Robert Mondavi brand intended to give good quality at a good price—good value, in other words. And this Cab does, with solid fruit flavours and nice balance. It's medium bodied and dry, and goes very well with burgers and grilled red meats.

NOTES

....

....

....

....

....

CHILE

CHILE PRODUCES MANY of the best-value red wines in the LCBO. They tend to be bold and full of flavour and include Carmenère (Chile's signature variety), Cabernet Sauvignon, Merlot, Syrah (Shiraz), and Pinot Noir, as well as some excellent blends.

What makes Chile such a good source for quality red wine? Climate and location are the keys. Most Chilean wine regions are in warm, sun soaked valleys such as Maipo, Aconcagua, and Colchagua. They're all well represented among the wines here. As Chile's wines gain the following they deserve and sales increase, expect prices to do the same. In the meantime, enjoy Chile's reds for their great quality and value.

Calama Merlot 2006

★ ★ ★

DO CENTRAL VALLEY $9.65   (612440)

This is a good example of the bottled value that pours out of Chile these days. It's a straightforward and unpretentious Merlot. It's not dreaming of being Pétrus when it grows up, and it's comfortable in its own skin—or out of its skin, in the case of the grapes. Look for good flavour intensity and attractive, refreshing texture in this dry and medium-bodied bargain. Drink it with red meats, burgers, or pizza.

NOTES

....
....
....
....

Caliterra Reserva Merlot 2006

★ ★ ★ ½

DO COLCHAGUA VALLEY $11.85   (466482)

Chile is well known for its big-flavoured, big-boned reds, and many Chilean Merlots fit the profile. This one is dry and medium bodied with firm tannins, so drink it with red meat cooked rare or medium-rare, which will cut through them. Then you'll discover the rich, teeth-staining, dense fruit flavours lurking below. Make sure you brush well before you go out after dinner.

NOTES

....
....
....
....

Carmen Merlot 2006

★ ★ ★

DO CENTRAL VALLEY $10.95   (248625)

This is a well-made, straightforward Merlot that's a versatile addition to your table. You can pair it with chicken or pork, with a veal chop or a steak, and it will also go down nicely with a burger or a pizza. It's dry and medium bodied and has solid flavours with light tannins. How can you go wrong? By serving it with one of those shrimp rings, which will lose all flavour against this Merlot.

NOTES

....
....
....
....

Carmen Reserve Cabernet Sauvignon 2005

★ ★ ★ ★ ½

DO MAIPO VALLEY $16.90 (358309)

If you like your red wine big and somewhat brash, with in-your-face fruitiness and a full-bodied, mouth-filling texture, you should test drive this. The flavours are saturating and flood your taste buds, while the wine seems to swell in your mouth. At the same time, it has the complexity and structure to handle the weight. It's full bodied, dry and has decent tannic grip, and will overwhelm anything but well-seasoned red meats.

NOTES

....

....

....

Carmen Reserve Carmenère/Cabernet Sauvignon 2005

★ ★ ★ ★

DO MAIPO VALLEY $16.90 (439166)

Some Chilean winemakers think the Carmenère grape needs a little Cabernet Sauvignon to give it structure and complexity. It works with this wine, a blend that delivers robust and intense fruit flavours with a similar texture. It's a big, bold red that's fruit forward, mouth filling, and dry. It needs food that's equally bold and full of flavour, so open it when you're serving a pepper steak or other well-seasoned red meat.

NOTES

....

....

....

....

Casillero del Diablo Cabernet Sauvignon 2007

★ ★ ★ ½

DO CENTRAL VALLEY $12.85 (278416)

Concha y Toro, one of Chile's major wine producers, came up with a winner in this Casillero del Diablo range. They're all good- and better-value wines. The Cabernet Sauvignon delivers a solid flavour profile with quite decent complexity and a nice tanginess in the texture. It's dry, with light-medium tannins, and is a natural for grilled red meats.

NOTES

....

....

....

....

....

Casillero del Diablo Carmenère 2007

★ ★ ★ ★ ½

DO CENTRAL VALLEY $12.95   (620666)

Is it a coincidence that a wine named for "The Devil's Cellar" was given a product code that included the numbers 666? And what was it the devil called, when he tried to lure a victim into his cellar? "Carmenère!" This example of Chile's iconic grape is full of fruit power, but well defined and textured. It's medium-to-full in body, and has an edgy tanginess that invites food. Send in a piece of grilled red meat.

NOTES

Casillero del Diablo Shiraz 2007

★ ★ ★ ½

DO CENTRAL VALLEY $12.95   (568055)

This range of wines is named for a cellar at the Concha y Toro winery. The story goes that in order to deter workers from going into the cellar to drink wine, the owner told them it was inhabited by the devil. Too bad for them if they missed out on the likes of this, an intensely flavoured, well-balanced red that's dry, tangy textured, and lightly tannic. It goes nicely with barbecued red meats.

NOTES

Concha y Toro 'Marques de Casa Concha' Cabernet Sauvignon 2005

★ ★ ★ ★ ½

DO MAIPO VALLEY $19.95   (337238)

[Vintages Essential] Concha y Toro produces huge volumes of wine that achieve quality across the board, but this is one of their limited-production brands. The grapes come from a single vineyard (always considered a plus) and the wine is oak-aged for 14 months. What you get for a very good price is an elegant, well-structured red with layers of flavours and a super-lative texture. Serve it with a good cut of red meat, cooked no more than medium-rare.

NOTES

★ ★ ★ ★

Cono Sur Merlot 2007

DO CENTRAL VALLEY $9.95 (457176)

Cono Sur manages its vineyards in a sustainable way and even uses a flock of geese to take care of the insects that harm the vines. The problem is the geese also like grapes and have to be removed to a fenced pond as harvest approaches. Enjoy this Merlot's ripe fruit flavours and tangy texture. It's dry with moderate tannins, and it goes well with grilled red meats and pork.

NOTES

....

....

....

....

....

★ ★ ★ ★ ½

Cono Sur Pinot Noir 2007

DO CENTRAL VALLEY $10.45 (341602)

Cono Sur is by far Chile's biggest producer of Pinot Noir. This one has the intense flavour you expect from a Chilean wine, but it's subtle enough to capture the classic textures and character of Pinot Noir. Look for concentrated flavours and a lively, food-friendly texture. Dry and medium-bodied, it has light tannins and goes very well with grilled salmon or lamb.

NOTES

....

....

....

★ ★ ★ ★ ½

Cono Sur Shiraz 2007

DO COLCHAGUA VALLEY $9.95 (64295)

This blends Shiraz (85 percent) with Malbec, Carmenère, Cabernet Sauvignon, and Pinot Noir. The result is a medium-bodied, dry red with rich flavours that are dense and remarkably (for this price) complex. It has light-to-moderate tannins and a quite tangy texture. This is an excellent buy and a great choice for grilled red meats and hearty vegetarian stews.

NOTES

....

....

....

....

★ ★ ★ ★ ★ **Cousiño-Macul 'Antiguas Reservas' Cabernet Sauvignon 2006**

DO MAIPO VALLEY $15.45   (212993)

This winery is located not far from Santiago, Chile's capital city, and you can visit its original cellars and buildings. This popular Cabernet Sauvignon is a real delight. It delivers gorgeous intense and layered flavours that work seamlessly with the smooth, rich and slightly tangy texture. It's medium bodied and dry, with moderate tannins, and is the perfect wine for a rack of lamb or a fine cut of beef.

NOTES

....

....

....

★ ★ ★ ★ ½ **Errazuriz Carmenère 2007**

DO ACONCAGUA VALLEY $13.80   (016238)

The Carmenère grape takes longer than almost any other variety to ripen fully, so it does best in regions with long growing seasons. This assertive Carmenère, from one of Chile's warmer valleys, delivers powerful and intense flavours and a plush, tangy, and mouth-filling texture. It's a touch on the fat side (low in acidity) and is a great wine for grilled lamb or beef.

NOTES

....

....

....

★ ★ ★ ★ ★ **Errazuriz 'Max Reserva' Shiraz 2006**

DO ACONCAGUA VALLEY $17.75   (614750)

You'd have to be mad not to try this Max. Just stick your nose in the glass and get a whiff of those aromas. Then take a small mouthful and appreciate the concentrated flavours . . . hold it there, and think about them. Ponder the elegant and rich texture, and feel the drying tannins. Then sigh. Then fill up your glass, cut into that juicy cut of red meat, and get on with living.

NOTES

....

....

....

145

Errazuriz Shiraz 2007

★ ★ ★ ★

DO RAPEL VALLEY $13.80   (604066)

If Shiraz were a movie star, it would be on the front page of *Variety*, the
Hollywood paper that could double as a wine report. Shiraz is the star
grape of the last 15 years, and it can make big and delicious wines like this.
Fruit-forward, dry, medium- to full-bodied, and saturated with flavour,
the wine is moderately tannic, and you'll enjoy it with grilled red meat.

NOTES

....
....
....
....
....

Espiritu de Chile Cabernet Sauvignon 2006

★ ★ ★ ½

DO CENTRAL VALLEY $10.95   (60657)

It might be a bit over the top to think of this wine as embodying the spirit
of Chile, but it does represent the country insofar as it's well-made wine
at a very good price. What you get here is a rich and tangy red that might
be more generic than Cabernet but is good-value drinking, nonetheless.
It's dry medium bodied, and fruity, and goes well with pizza, burgers, red
meats, and flavourful cheeses.

NOTES

....
....
....
....

Julio Bouchon Reserva Cabernet Sauvignon 2006

★ ★ ★ ★

DO MAULE VALLEY $8.70   (531764)

If you're after a very reasonably priced, well-made red wine that has good
complexity and quality, this might be just what you're looking for. The
fruit flavours are nicely layered and the texture is quite plush and tangy.
It's medium bodied and dry and has light tannins. Really, what more do
you want at this price? Serve it with a wide range of dishes, from burgers
to steak.

NOTES

....
....
....
....

Mont Gras Reserva Cabernet Sauvignon 2007

★ ★ ★ ★ ½

DO COLCHAGUA VALLEY $11.80   (619205)

So much excellent Cabernet Sauvignon comes our way from Chile, and a lot of it seems totally underpriced. This one, for example, delivers quality across the board. The fruit is concentrated, complex, and beautifully layered as it emanates from a sweet core. The texture is smooth, generous, and refreshing in its balance. It's medium bodied and dry, with a bit of a tannic grip, and it's a natural for grilled red meat.

NOTES

....

....

....

....

Pérez Cruz Reserva Cabernet Sauvignon 2006

★ ★ ★ ★ ★

DO MAIPO VALLEY $14.95   (694208)

[Vintages Essential] This is a totally opulent Cabernet Sauvignon, verging on the decadent. It's full of delicious layered flavours, and it's stylish to boot. You can smell the rich aromas as you pour the wine into your glass. The texture is full, smooth, and generous, and for all its complex fruitiness, this is a dry wine with moderate tannins. It's perfect with well-seasoned red meat, like lamb with garlic and rosemary.

NOTES

....

....

....

....

Punta Nogal Shiraz 2007

★ ★ ★

DO RAPEL VALLEY $9.70   (619197)

Shiraz like this can give Australia, which has become the byword for Shiraz, a run for its money. And at this price, the cash won't run out soon. This is a fruit-forward Shiraz with uncomplicated, fairly intense flavours and a round, smooth texture with a little tanginess. It's dry, medium bodied, and perfect for drinking with juicy burgers and spicy foods, such as barbecued ribs.

NOTES

....

....

....

....

Santa Alicia Reserve Carmenère 2005
★ ★ ★ ★
DO MAIPO VALLEY $11.95   (309302)

No wonder so many people rally to Carmenère once they first taste the grape. It has everything that's popular: fruitiness, power, quite high alcohol, and price. This one is a good example. You get deep and quite rich flavours and a mouth-saturating and tangy texture. It's fruity and fruit forward, but it has balancing complexity and is medium bodied. At this price, it's everything you want (and more) for grilled red meats or aged hard cheese.

NOTES

Santa Carolina Cabernet Sauvignon/Merlot 2006
★ ★ ★ ★
DO CENTRAL VALLEY $9.25   (245282)

Santa Carolina is getting it right, with a series of well-priced and well-made entries on the LCBO list. This blend delivers what you might expect, but in an attractive and affordable way. The flavours are clearly defined and have decent complexity, and the texture is tangy and appealing. This is medium bodied, very dry, and lightly tannic, and it goes well with herbed chicken or with burgers and red meats.

NOTES

Santa Carolina Reserva Cabernet Sauvignon 2007
★ ★ ★ ★
DO COLCHAGUA VALLEY $12.80   (275925)

Here's a Chilean Cabernet Sauvignon that expresses all that's attractive about easy-drinking, affordable wines, while adding value in the form of complexity. The flavours are intense and interesting, and the texture is spicy and fresh. It's medium bodied and dry, with tannins that you'll feel on your gums, and it's a natural for red meat dishes of many kinds.

NOTES

Santa Carolina Reserva Merlot 2006

★ ★ ★ ★

DO COLCHAGUA VALLEY $12.80   (324590)

It's worth saying again that many of the best-value wines come from regions that are underrated. This Merlot is a good example. It delivers tangy flavours that are concentrated and quite complex, and a solid, spicy texture. Medium-bodied, dry, and moderately tannic, it's well made and goes perfectly with a wide range of generously seasoned meat and vegetarian dishes.

NOTES
....
....
....
....
....

Santa Digna Reserve Cabernet Sauvignon 2005

★ ★ ★ ★ ½

DO CENTRAL VALLEY $14.95   (177451)

[Vintages Essential] The Central Valley is a long, warm suntrap that runs north-south between the Andes and Chile's coastal range. It produces the grapes for this medium-bodied 100 percent Cabernet. The wine has a tangy texture that goes nicely with well-seasoned red meat, like a New York strip loin with a shake or two of steak spice. It's dry, with moderate tannins, and delivers concentrated flavours of ripe fruit.

NOTES
....
....
....
....

Santa Rita Reserva Cabernet Sauvignon 2006

★ ★ ★ ★

DO MAIPO VALLEY $13.95   (253872)

Santa Rita has one of the most beautiful estates in Chile, and you get only a suggestion of it from the sketch on the bottle's label. What's more important, though, is what's inside. This is a very attractive Cabernet Sauvignon, with concentrated and complex flavours and a layered, generous, and tangy texture. It's dry and medium bodied with light tannins, and a great choice for red meats.

NOTES
....
....
....

Tarapaca Cabernet Sauvignon 2007

★ ★ ★

DO MAIPO VALLEY $9.80   (249599)

Tarapaca (the accent is on the final *a*) has produced an easy-drinking
Cabernet at a price that makes it ideal for large crowds around the barbecue. This is simply a well-made and straightforward red that delivers ripe
fruit flavours and a tangy texture. It's light- to medium-bodied, fruity but
dry, and has light tannins. It's the sort of wine that works with just about
any grilled meat, not to mention pizza and burgers.

NOTES

....

....

....

....

Tarapaca Reserva Carmenère 2006

★ ★ ★

DO MAIPO VALLEY $12.80   (64436)

This is an uncomplicated Carmenère but it's recognizable as the variety
that has become Chile's signature grape. The wine has quite dense and
rich flavours, not with a lot of complexity but enjoyable nonetheless. The
texture is rich and tangy, and the drying tannins are quite prominent. It's
dry and medium bodied, and makes a great partner for juicy hamburgers
and grilled red meats.

NOTES

....

....

....

....

Trio Cabernet Sauvignon/Shiraz/Cabernet Franc 2006

★ ★ ★ ★

DO MAIPO VALLEY $14.95   (433912)

This is an unusual blend but it really works. What you get is full-on fruit
flavours that are intense and deep, yet exhibit good complexity and layer-
ing. It's dry, with medium tannic grip, and it offers a generous, mouth-
filling texture that's tangy and has an attractive note of rusticity. This
blend calls for food that's substantial in weight and flavour, so try it with
something like a pepper steak.

NOTES

....

....

....

....

Trio Merlot/Carmenère/Cabernet Sauvignon 2006

★ ★ ★ ★

DO RAPEL VALLEY $14.85   (433920)

Concha y Toro's "Trio" series features wines that are blends of three varieties, or of grapes from three regions. This mostly Merlot blend delivers a plush texture with intensely concentrated flavours that come on in waves of complexity. It's totally dry, and leaves your mouth with an astringent feel. It's medium- to full-bodied and is an obvious choice for hearty red meat dishes.

NOTES

....

....

....

....

FRANCE

FRANCE IS ONE OF THE WORLD'S LARGEST and most important wine producers and has scores of wines in the LCBO. For many years, French wine was widely believed to be the best in the world, and Bordeaux and Burgundies were held up as the only wines worth drinking if you wanted to taste excellence. That's no longer so, as wine lovers have discovered the great wines made elsewhere. But France continues to make high-quality and value-priced wine, as this list shows.

French wine labels carry some terms worth knowing. Wines labelled *Appellation d'Origine Contrôlée* (abbreviated AOC here) are ones in the highest quality classification in France. They're made under tight rules that regulate such things as the grape varieties that can be used in each region.

Wines labelled *Vin de Pays* are regional wines made with fewer restrictions. They must be good quality, but producers have much more flexibility in the varieties they can use and how much wine they can make. *Vin de Pays d'Oc* is by far the most important of the Vins de Pays wines.

Antonin Rodet Côtes du Rhône 2006

★ ★ ★ ★ ★

AOC CÔTES DU RHÔNE $13.15   (8979)

Antonin Rodet started off making wine in Burgundy in 1875, and the winery now produces wines under various labels in many other French regions. This Côtes du Rhône has an attractive texture—juicy and generous and ideal for food. The flavours have good depth, and the wine is dry and medium bodied, pitched just right for your meal, especially veal or lamb, but turkey or chicken, too.

NOTES

....

....

....

....

Azzaro Merlot 2006

★ ★ ★ ½

VIN DE PAYS D'OC $14.30   (64600)

This winery is owned by Loris Azzaro, the French designer. What's next? Chanel Chardonnay? Boss Barbera? But fear not, it's not all about the name; this Merlot has been well designed and will fit you to a T. It's quite a plush little number, with nicely formed flavours and an attractive texture (if not textile). Wear this next time you have a date with a grilled veal chop.

NOTES

....

....

....

....

Baron Philippe de Rothschild Merlot 2007

★ ★ ★ ★

VIN DE PAYS D'OC $10.95   (407544)

Merlot originated in Bordeaux, but it's a great traveller and has become one of the "international varieties." Then again, southern France, where the grapes for this particular wine grew, isn't far from Bordeaux. They show their warm growing conditions in ripe fruit flavours with depth and weight. They're also complex and spicy. This is dry and medium bodied with light tannins, and it's excellent with spicy or peppery red meats.

NOTES

....

....

....

....

Bouchard Aîné & Fils Pinot Noir 2006

★ ★ ★ ★

AOC BOURGOGNE $17.05   (665406)

Although many Burgundies (most from smaller appellations within the broader Burgundy region) command high prices, you can still get good quality at a reasonable price. Like this one. It delivers attractive, bright aromas and flavours that have good complexity and are nicely layered. It's medium bodied and dry, with a solid, tangy texture and goes well with duck breast, lamb, and other densely flavoured dishes.

NOTES

....

....

....

....

Bouchard Père & Fils Beaujolais-Villages 2006

★ ★ ★ ½

AOC BEAUJOLAIS-VILLAGES $12.95   (665448)

It's easy to forget that Beaujolais is part of Burgundy, but here's a reminder: a Beaujolais-Villages from a producer known for its Burgundies. This is in a classic style, light- to medium-bodied with somewhat complex and vibrant fruit flavours, and a bright, tangy, and crisp texture. It's a very good candidate for turkey and cranberries or baked ham.

NOTES

....

....

....

....

....

Bouchard Père & Fils Mâcon 2006

★ ★ ★ ½

AOC MÂCON $12.85   (41350)

Mâcon lies at the southern end of the main Burgundy region and makes red wines from Pinot Noir and Gamay varieties. This one gives you quite concentrated and ripe flavours with some complexity, and a fairly generous, mouth-filling, and smooth texture. It's medium bodied and dry, with a light tannic grip, and goes well with lamb or veal chops, or with grilled salmon.

NOTES

....

....

....

....

....

Caves des Papes Côtes du Rhône 2006

★ ★ ★ ½

This is a blend of Grenache, Syrah, and Mourvèdre, sometimes abbreviated "GSM" as it's a common trio, not only in France but as far afield as Australia. This example is medium bodied and dry, with tannins that are still gripping well. It shows good, solid fruit flavours and a fairly plump, mouth-filling texture. Drink it with red meat cooked no more than medium-rare or with two-year-old cheddar cheese.

NOTES

....

....

....

....

Caves des Papes Côtes du Ventoux 2006

★ ★ ★ ★

AOC CÔTES DU VENTOUX $11.45   (569095)

Mont Ventoux is a mountain in Provence, one of the highest in the region and sometimes called the "Giant of Provence." This medium-bodied Grenache-Syrah blend isn't exactly a giant of a wine, but it delivers lovely sweet flavours and an attractive juicy texture. It's dry with firm tannins, and makes a great partner for veal and beef.

NOTES

....

....

....

....

....

Cellier des Dauphins 'Carte Noir' Côtes du Rhône 2006

★ ★ ★

AOC CÔTES DU RHÔNE $10.95   (110197)

The broad Côtes du Rhône appellation in the southern Rhône Valley, not too far from the Mediterranean, churns out vast volumes of wine, ranging from the exquisite to the very mediocre. This one is sort of mid-range: well made and well priced. Look for good fruit flavours that are solid and straightforward, and a tangy texture. It's medium bodied, dry, and versatile; just the thing for mid-week barbecues or pizza.

NOTES

....

....

....

....

Château de Gourgazaud 2006

★ ★ ★ ½

AOC MINERVOIS $13.20   (22384)

This is one of the LCBO's veterans, and it owes its longevity not to inertia but to the fact that it delivers quality and value, vintage after vintage. The aromas and flavours are quite intense and decently complex, and the texture is rich, smooth, and mouth filling. Add medium weight, good balance, and drying tannins, and you have a well-built red that goes beautifully with roast or grilled red meats.

NOTES

....

....

....

....

....

Château des Laurets 2005

★ ★ ★ ★

AOC PUISSEGUIN-ST-ÉMILION $20.60   (371401)

Puisseguin-St-Émilion is one of the satellite regions of well-known St-Émilion on Bordeaux's right bank. Merlot is the major grape variety there, and this is a well-made Merlot-dominant blend with concentrated and complex fruit flavours, great balance, and fine tannins. It's dry and medium bodied, and goes nicely with well-seasoned red meat dishes.

NOTES

....

....

....

....

Château de Terrefort-Quancard 2003

★ ★ ★ ★

AOC BORDEAUX SUPÉRIEUR $15.85   (145110)

The laws regulating Bordeaux Supérieur wines are a bit tighter than the rules that control wines labelled simply "Bordeaux." This well-made blend (70 percent Merlot, along with Cabernets Sauvignon and Franc) is medium bodied and dry, with light tannins. The flavours are attractive and bright, with some depth and complexity, and the texture is smooth and fine grained. Serve it with roast chicken, ham, or pork.

NOTES

....

....

....

....

Château Pey La Tour 'Réserve du Château' 2005

★ ★ ★ ★ ½

AOC BORDEAUX SUPÉRIEUR $22.95   (925859)

[Vintages Essential] Bordeaux has special status among wines, and here's evidence that you don't need to take out a second mortgage to taste a good one. This Merlot-dominant blend (89 percent, with 8 percent Cabernet Sauvignon and 3 percent Petit Verdot) is smooth and clean textured, with complex and concentrated flavours. It's medium bodied, dry with firm tannins, and has terrific balance. It's just lovely, and an excellent dancing partner for red meats.

NOTES

....
....
....
....

Chat-en-Oeuf 2005

★ ★ ★ ★

AOC CÔTES DU VENTOUX $14.30   (665596)

The name is a play on Châteauneuf (du Pape) and the label shows a cat (*chat*) sitting on an egg (*oeuf*). Whoever hatched this idea deserves praise, as it's one of the best pieces of marketing from France I've seen in ages. The wine is good quality, too. It's a dry, medium-bodied blend of Grenache and Shiraz that delivers quite intense flavours and a juicy, refreshing texture. Purr-fect for grilled red meats.

NOTES

....
....
....

Christian Moueix Merlot 2005

★ ★ ★ ★

AOC BORDEAUX $15.95   (961227)

[Vintages Essential] More and more French wines are being labelled by grape variety as well as region, since non-French consumers identify wines that way. This Bordeaux labelled "Merlot" is an example. But the wine itself is unchanged. Here you get a well-structured red that delivers solid and quite complex flavours, and a mid-weight, smooth, and appealing texture. Drink it with grilled or roasted red meats or even with roast turkey.

NOTES

....
....
....
....

Croix du Mayne 2004

★ ★ ★ ½

AOC CAHORS $17.70 (28548)

Cahors is a small wine region in southwestern France. It's an original Malbec region, and its wine laws require a minimum of 70 percent Malbec in an AOC Cahors wine. This one delivers intense, complex, and layered fruit flavours. It's medium bodied, with a tangy texture and light tannins, making it a pretty versatile food wine. Drink it with red meats or hearty vegetarian dishes.

NOTES

....

....

....

Domaine de Sérame Reserve Cabernet Sauvignon 2005

★ ★ ★ ★

VIN DE PAYS D'OC $14.15 (35006)

The label points out that this estate dates back to the 12th century. Very nice, but frankly, it wouldn't matter to me if its history spanned only a couple of decades, as long as its wine tasted like this. With well-layered flavours and a tangy and refreshing texture, it's a natural for simply prepared grilled or roasted red meats. The tannins grip nicely, and it's dry and medium bodied.

NOTES

....

....

....

....

E. Guigal Côtes du Rhône 2004

★ ★ ★ ★ ½

AOC CÔTES DU RHÔNE $18.25 (259721)

There's so much mediocre Côtes du Rhône about that it's important to know which wines stand out in quality. No doubt at all that this, from one of the most respected producers in the Rhône Valley, holds its own. It carries its concentrated flavour with lightness and elegance, and the tangy texture is stylish. Medium-bodied, astringently dry, and moderately tannic, it's an excellent choice for red meats.

NOTES

....

....

....

Fat Bastard Shiraz 2007

★★★★

VIN DE PAYS D'OC $14.85   (563122)

Fat Bastard paved the way for edgy brands that the authorities once worried might offend the delicate sensitivities of Ontario wine lovers. Now it's an established wine whose solid, rich, and spicy dark fruit flavours and tangy texture have a good following. It's medium bodied and dry with firm tannins, and it teams perfectly with well-seasoned lamb or beef.

NOTES
....
....
....
....

La Fiole du Pape Châteauneuf-du-Pape

★★★★

AOC CHÂTEAUNEUF-DU-PAPE $40.05   (12286)

[Non-vintage] You can't miss the bottle. It's gnarled and twisted, with a rough, gritty texture as if it's been in a fire. But the wine's in very good shape. It's a stylish red that has good structure and food-friendly balance. Look for concentrated flavours with spicy accents and a tangy texture. It's medium bodied and dry, with moderate tannins. Serve it with grilled or roasted red meats.

NOTES
....
....
....
....

Fortant de France Merlot 2006

★★★

VIN DE PAYS D'OC $9.90   (293969)

Fortant is a brand of Robert Skalli, a producer that turns out a wide range of good-value wines. This Merlot, from the Pays d'Oc region that's so well represented in this book, is dry and medium bodied and pairs nicely with roast chicken, red meats, or tomato-based pasta. It has a lively and tangy texture, quite vibrant flavours, and very light tannins.

NOTES
....
....
....
....

★ ★ ★ ★ ## François Chauvenet 'Grand Pavois' Beaujolais 2006
AOC BEAUJOLAIS $11.75 (6114)

Too many people think that Beaujolais isn't a serious wine, that it's pale in colour, simple in flavour, and lacking in interest. This one proves they're wrong. It has bright fruit flavours with plenty of complexity. The texture is mouth filling and juicy, and it's light-to-medium in body. This all makes it a good choice when you're eating roast ham, pork, or turkey.

NOTES
....
....
....
....
....

★ ★ ★ ★ ## François Labet 'Dame Alix' Côtes du Rhône 2006
AOC CÔTES DU RHÔNE $10.65 (630657)

This is a blend of Grenache, Syrah, and Mourvèdre, three of the classic grapes of this region that spreads across a broad swath east of the River Rhône near the Mediterranean. It has dense and concentrated flavours, with a smooth texture. Dry and medium-bodied, with moderate tannins, it has both style and power. Drink it with well-seasoned food like a hearty meat stew.

NOTES
....
....
....
....

★ ★ ★ ½ ## Georges Duboeuf Beaujolais 2007
AOC BEAUJOLAIS $12.15 (212480)

Georges Duboeuf is the name most of us associate with Beaujolais, and there are several of his wines from the Beaujolais region in the LCBO—and in this book. This is a popular wine that offers bright, vibrant fruit flavours and a lively texture. It's dry and medium bodied, and goes well with chicken, turkey, and ham. It's not a bad idea to chill the wine first; give it, say, 10 to 15 minutes in the fridge.

NOTES
....
....
....
....

★ ★ ★ ★

Georges Duboeuf Beaujolais-Villages 2007

AOC BEAUJOLAIS-VILLAGES $12.85   (122077)

The "Villages" add-on to Beaujolais indicates that the grapes were grown in regions around specific villages that are reputed to produce grapes of superior quality. But note that there's not much difference in price between this and the previous listing. The flavours here are quite concentrated and more complex than in the generic Beaujolais, and the texture is bigger and spicier. It goes nicely with well-seasoned white meats.

NOTES

....

....

....

....

★ ★ ★ ★

Georges Duboeuf Brouilly 2007

AOC BROUILLY $16.85   (70540)

The tall bottle stands out on the LCBO shelves, and the wine stands out, too. It's from one of the sub-regions of Beaujolais that have been designated as producers of superior wine. The fruit here is quite lovely—concentrated and fairly complex, and it's generous and juicy in its texture. You can drink this with roast turkey and all the trimmings, but chill the wine down a little first.

NOTES

....

....

....

....

★ ★ ★ ½

Jeanjean Merlot 2007

VIN DE PAYS D'OC $10.45   (582130)

Vintage after vintage, the Pays d'Oc produces both quantity and remarkable quality. This Merlot delivers quite concentrated and defined fruit flavours and an edgy, tangy texture. It's dry and just on the lighter side of medium bodied. It's all balanced and makes a versatile wine for food. Drink it with pizza, burgers, red meats, or chicken.

NOTES

....

....

....

....

....

Joseph Drouhin Côte de Beaune-Villages 2006
★ ★ ★ ★

AOC CÔTE DE BEAUNE-VILLAGES $19.95   (47845)

This is from a region near beautiful Beaune, a wine town if ever there was one. It's studded with wineries, wine shops, wine bars, and excellent restaurants. Drouhin has made a lovely Pinot Noir, with intense and layered fruit and a rich, smooth but slightly edgy texture. It's dry and medium bodied and goes very well with a meal that includes mushroom risotto.

NOTES
....
....
....
....
....

Louis Bernard Côtes du Rhône 2006
★ ★ ★ ★

AOC CÔTES DU RHÔNE $10.85   (581645)

Louis Bernard now has its headquarters in a 12th-century fortified convent close to Avignon, and the company is carefully conserving the building and grounds. This Côtes du Rhône, mainly Grenache and Syrah, offers a lovely texture that's rich and juicy, and shows off the solid fruit flavours. It's dry, with good firm tannins, and goes well with roast turkey.

NOTES
....
....
....
....
....

Louis Jadot 'Combe aux Jacques' Beaujolais-Villages 2007
★ ★ ★ ½

AOC BEAUJOLAIS-VILLAGES $17.95   (365924)

[Vintages Essential] Light in tannins, Beaujolais (which is made from the Gamay grape) is often a good choice for anyone who finds that red wines lead to a headache. This one is quite classic: medium bodied, dry, full of bright fruit flavours with limited complexity, and a vibrant and refreshing texture. You can serve it a little chilled, especially outside in the summer. Drink it with roast or grilled chicken or with roast turkey.

NOTES
....
....
....
....

★ ★ ★ ★ ½ **Mommessin Châteauneuf-du-Pape 2006**
AOC CHÂTEAUNEUF-DU-PAPE $29.70   (42242)

The vineyards in this famous wine region are full of big smooth rocks (*galets*). They absorb heat during the day and release it at night, helping the grapes to fully ripen. This is a gorgeous wine that delivers generous amounts of juicy, ripe fruit flavours, full-bodied weight, and a creamy texture. The acid-to-fruit balance is excellent. It's quite stylish and is an excellent wine to drink with thick slices of medium-rare roast beef.

NOTES

....

....

....

....

★ ★ ★ ★ **Mommessin 'Les Epices' Côtes du Rhône 2006**
AOC CÔTES DU RHÔNE $11.40   (14829)

This is a blend of four grapes—Grenache, Carignane, Cinsault, and Syrah—grown in the broad southern end of the Rhône Valley. Each adds its own strength to the wine, and the result is fairly impressive. The flavours are quite bold—assertive, but not aggressive—and there's very good balancing acidity showing through. It's dry with moderate tannins, and makes an excellent partnership with hearty red meats and stews.

NOTES

....

....

....

....

★ ★ ★ ★ **Mouton Cadet Réserve Rouge 2006**
AOC MÉDOC $16.95   (52274)

No need to be sheepish about putting this on your table, even if you're serving lamb—which this wine happens to go with very well. It has bright flavours and a juicy texture, and it's dry and medium bodied with light tannins. You don't *have* to serve it with lamb just because of the name (*mouton* means "sheep"); it also goes well with chicken, veal, and beef. It's a step up from the Mouton Cadet Rouge (i.e., non-Réserve), which itself is good value.

NOTES

....

....

....

Patriarche Pinot Noir 2006
★ ★ ★ ★
VIN DE PAYS D'OC $9.95   (522649)

The big Pays d'Oc wine region runs along France's western Mediterranean coast. It's pretty warm during the growing season, and not the sort of climate you'd expect cool-loving Pinot Noir to thrive in. But here, concentrated flavours are well complemented by acidity to give a tangy and refreshing texture. Dry and medium-bodied, it's a great choice for duck, lamb, or mushroom-based vegetarian dishes.

NOTES

Paul Jaboulet Aîné 'Parallèle 45' Côtes du Rhône 2006
★ ★ ★ ★
AOC CÔTES DU RHÔNE $16.35   (332304)

The name comes from the 45th latitudinal parallel, which passes just two kilometres south of Jaboulet's cellars. A compelling blend of Syrah and Grenache, it's a rich, intense wine, with layered fruit flavours and lots of tanginess in the texture. It's dry, medium- to full-bodied, and has pretty firm tannins. Pair it with grilled lamb.

NOTES

Perrin Réserve Côtes du Rhône 2005
★ ★ ★ ★ ★
AOC CÔTES DU RHÔNE $14.95   (363457)

[Vintages Essential] Tremendous value pours from this bottle, vintage after vintage. It's a blend of Grenache, Syrah, Mourvèdre, and Cinsault, and it's made by the producer of Château de Beaucastel, an iconic wine from Châteauneuf-du-Pape. This one delivers rich, luscious flavours with an astonishingly intense, smooth, and mouth-filling texture. Dry and well-structured, with good tannic grip, it's a great choice for grilled or roasted red meats.

NOTES

Rafale Merlot 2006

★ ★ ★

VIN DE PAYS D'OC $8.15   (526897)

You really can't go wrong with this wine at this price. It's not very complex, not very anything, in fact, but it's a perfectly decent red to serve at parties and barbecues and with casual mid-week meals, such as hamburgers. It's very dry (it leaves your mouth with that furry, tannic sensation) and delivers solid, fruity flavours, a smooth and mouth-filling texture, and pretty good balance.

NOTES

....

....

....

....

Ted the Mule Syrah/Grenache 2006

★ ★ ★ ★ ½

AOC CÔTES DU VENTOUX $12.95   (665463)

The name is a play on *tête de mule*, which means "stubborn." You'd be an ass not to try this wine, as it delivers full-flavoured and juicy sweet fruit, along with quite assertive spiciness. It's dry and medium bodied with a tangy texture, and it's delicious with grilled lamb chops, but you can pair it just as well with roast chicken or barbecued ribs.

NOTES

....

....

....

....

La Vieille Ferme Côtes du Ventoux 2006

★ ★ ★ ½

AOC CÔTES DU VENTOUX $11.85   (263640)

This is a blend of four southern French grape varieties—Grenache, Syrah, Mourvèdre, and Cinsault—grown high on the slopes of Mont Ventoux. They find cooler conditions there, and the flavours here are concentrated and rich, but not too intense. The texture is tangy, and you'll feel drying tannins. You might want to tame them by drinking this with red meat, cooked medium-rare at most, or with aged hard cheese, like two-year-old cheddar.

NOTES

....

....

....

....

Yvon Mau Shiraz 2007

★ ★ ★

VIN DE PAYS DE L'AUDE $9.45   (621979)

The Aude wine region lies in southwest France, near the Mediterranean and the border with Spain. This Shiraz shows the warm environment in its ripe fruit flavours. It's medium bodied and bone dry, and it has a tangy texture that invites a mouthful of food. You'll happily down a glass or two with hamburgers, but it goes equally well with kebabs and red meat in general.

NOTES

....

....

....

....

....

GREECE

THE HOT GROWING CONDITIONS IN GREECE make for full-flavoured reds. Although many are produced from native grape varieties, notably Agiorgitiko (sometimes called St. George), international varieties such as Cabernet Sauvignon are also making headway. An AOC-designated wine from Greece means that it complies with the laws regulating wine quality.

★ ★ ★ ★   **Hatzimichalis Cabernet Sauvignon 2004**

This is a powerful and very attractive blend of Cabernet Sauvignon, Merlot, and Cabernet Franc, all grapes associated with Bordeaux. Made in an international style, it has flavours that are bold and intense, and they're paralleled by the big, mouth-filling texture. This is a full-bodied blend, dry and still very tannic, so serve it with red meats cooked medium-rare at most, or with aged hard cheese, so as to soften the tannins.

NOTES

....

....

....

....

....

★ ★ ★ ½   **Kouros Agioritiko 2006**

AOC NEMEA $10.95   (144576)

Nemea is a wine region in the Peloponnese in southern Greece, known for its production of red wine, especially from the Agiorgitiko variety. This one has a tangy texture that points it towards food. The solid fruit flavours are enhanced with a little spiciness. It's dry and medium bodied, and is a good partner for well-seasoned beef, lamb, chicken, or pork kebabs.

NOTES

....

....

....

....

....

THE 500 BEST-VALUE WINES IN THE LCBO | 2009

ITALY

ITALY HAS LONG PRODUCED RED WINES from native grape varieties, but in recent years "international" varieties like Merlot and Cabernet Sauvignon have also been planted. There are many regional grapes, the best known being Sangiovese, originally from Tuscany and now grown and used in winemaking throughout Italy. Other important grapes are Nero d'Avola from Sicily and Primitivo from southern Italy.

The highest-quality classification of Italian wine, DOCG (*Denominazione di Origine Controllata e Garantita*), means a wine is made to stringent regulations and from specified grape varieties. So are the wines in the second-quality category, DOC (*Denominazione di Origine Controllata*). Wines labelled IGT (*Indicazione Geografica Tipica*) are made according to less stringent regulations and may use a wider range of grape varieties, but are often excellent in quality and value.

Bersano 'Costalunga' Barbera d'Asti 2005

★ ★ ★ ★

DOC BARBERA D'ASTI $12.15   (348680)

The Barbera grape variety comes from the Piedmont region and is Italy's second most-planted variety (after Sangiovese). It has naturally high acidity, which makes this an excellent wine for the tomato-based (and therefore somewhat acidic) dishes common in Italian cuisine. This Barbera has that acidity and is nicely complemented by rich, complex flavours. It's dry with a decent tannic grip.

NOTES
....
....
....
....

Bolla Amarone di Valpolicella Classico 2005

★ ★ ★ ★

DOC AMARONE DI VALPOLICELLA CLASSICO

$36.95   (352757)

Amarone is made by drying the grapes before pressing them for their juice. As the water evaporates and the grapes shrivel, the sugar and flavours are concentrated, making for an intense and richly structured wine. This one has it all, with dense and complex flavours and textures. It's dry and quite tannic, and you should pair it with rich red meat cooked medium-rare at most or with aged hard cheeses.

NOTES
....
....
....
....

Casal Thaulero Sangiovese 2007

★ ★ ★ ★

IGT TERRE DI CHIETI $7.10   (588996)

This is a very attractive Sangiovese. It has all the character you want from the grape—refreshing texture and fresh fruit flavour—but it has a bit more depth and complexity than most others around this low, low price. Look for bright flavours, a juicy texture, and medium body. It's dry with light tannins, and it goes well with spaghetti bolognese or vegetarian lasagna.

NOTES
....
....
....
....

Cent'Are Nero d'Avola 2005

★ ★ ★ ½

IGT SICILIA $14.95 (546192)

[Vintages Essential] The Nero d'Avola grape variety is native to Sicily and makes wines with intense flavours and colour. Cent'Are has been a popular Vintages Essential wine for years. It has concentrated flavours, is dry and medium bodied, and has moderate tannins. Drink this with tasty vegetarian dishes like portobello burgers.

NOTES
....
....
....
....
....

Cesari Amarone Classico 2004

★ ★ ★ ★ ½

DOC AMARONE DELLA VALPOLICELLA CLASSICO

$35.05 (426718)

This has the structure and concentration of flavours expected of a well-made Amarone. It's deep and broad, with layers of pungent, vibrant, and mature flavours that come on in waves. The texture is rich, tangy, mouth filling, and surprisingly lively. Dry, full-bodied, and delicious, this Amarone calls for substantial and well-seasoned red meat dishes.

NOTES
....
....
....
....

Cesari Merlot 2007

★ ★ ★ ½

IGT VENEZIE $7.45 (572453)

It sometimes seems odd that Italy, with so many indigenous grape varieties of its own, has rallied so strongly to the so-called "international varieties," such as Merlot. They tend to be made in the Italian style, with good structure and somewhat higher acidity to go with food. This straightforward Merlot has quite concentrated flavours and a good, refreshing texture. Drink it with pizza and tomato-based pasta.

NOTES
....
....
....
....

Citra Montepulciano d'Abruzzo 2007

★ ★ ★ ★

DOC MONTEPULCIANO D'ABRUZZO $7.25   (446633)

Like many Italian wine names, this combines a grape variety (Montepulciano) and a wine region (Abruzzo). It's a surprisingly well-made wine for the price. You get rich, concentrated flavours that flow through from start to finish. It might not be all that complex, but the texture is very attractive—tangy and refreshing, and ideal for grilled red meats and hearty tomato-based vegetarian stews.

NOTES

....

....

....

Citra Sangiovese 2007

★ ★ ★ ½

IGT TERRE DI CHIETI $7.25   (480756)

If you're ordering pizzas for a large party, consider serving this inexpensive red. Sangiovese is Italy's signature grape variety, mainly because it's the principal grape used in Chianti, the country's best-known wine. This one is not as complex as more expensive Chiantis, but its tangy and refreshing texture will play nicely off the tomato sauce, and it has enough stuff to cope with meats and cheese.

NOTES

....

....

....

Colli Berici 'i Basalti' Merlot 2006

★ ★ ★

DOC COLLI BERICI $8.55   (331801)

[1 Litre] Sealed with a screw cap and in a one-litre bottle, you might think this is cheap and nasty, just the sort of wine a budding or veteran wine snob would give a wide berth. In fact, it's inexpensive and well made. It has solid ripe fruit flavours, with a hint of sweetness. Medium-bodied, with a fruity, juicy texture, this is a wine to drink with spicy foods, like hot wings or ribs.

NOTES

....

....

....

Fabiano Valpolicella Classico 2005

★ ★ ★ ½

DOC VALPOLICELLA CLASSICO $14.85   (34058)

The label on this won't win you over. It might, in fact, tempt you to put the bottle back on the shelf. But wait! The wine inside could be just what you want to serve with osso bucco or a pasta dish tonight. It has solid, vibrant flavours and a medium-weight, tangy, and refreshing texture. Beyond that, it's quite astringently dry and only mildly tannic.

NOTES

Farnese Sangiovese 2007

★ ★ ★ ★

IGT DAUNIA $7.55   (512327)

When this wine first appeared in Ontario's liquor stores a few years ago, its price-quality combination made it an instant hit. It flew off the shelves, and the LCBO had trouble keeping it in stock. It's still very good value, even though the price has climbed a little. Look for bright and vibrant flavours, medium weight and a refreshing texture. You can't go wrong serving this with pizza and tomato-based pasta.

NOTES

Feudo Arancio Syrah 2005

★ ★ ★ ½

IGT SICILIA $11.80   (621730)

Given Sicily's warm climate, it's surprising that most of its wine production used to be white. Now the tables have turned (as have consumer preferences) towards red. This Sicilian Syrah delivers full flavours that are well paced and not too heavy, and a tangy texture. It's dry, has medium tannins, and is only just medium bodied. Drink it with roast chicken or pork, or with simply prepared red meats.

NOTES

Folonari Shiraz 2006

★ ★ ★ ★

IGT SICILY $12.95   (619494)

This is a Shiraz grown in Italy and showing the influences of both nearby southern France and far-off Australia. It's fruitier than a French *Syrah* (as Shiraz is called there) but has more structure and complexity than most Australian Shirazes at this price. Look for layers of concentrated flavour, a full and tangy texture, and drying tannins. It's an excellent choice for red meats.

NOTES

Folonari Valpolicella Classico Superiore Ripasso 2006

★ ★ ★ ★

DOC VALPOLICELLA CLASSICO SUPERIORE RIPASSO

$16.95   (481838)

Valpolicella Ripasso reds are more complex than straight Valpolicellas because the fermented wine is stored for two or three weeks in barrels with the grape skins left over from Recioto, a sweet red wine from the region. This Folonari Ripasso has stylish, dense, sweet fruit flavours with some complexity. It's dry and quite tannic, and goes nicely with well-seasoned red meats.

NOTES

Fontanafredda Barbera d'Alba Briccotondo 2005

★ ★ ★ ½

DOC BARBERA D'ALBA $12.35   (38174)

Barbera should be a more popular grape variety. It produces wines that are richly flavoured and refreshing and that go well with many Italian dishes or other foods that have a tomato base. This Barbera from the Alba region is slightly more than medium bodied, with refreshing, crisp, concentrated, and vibrant fruit flavours. It's nicely tannic and goes well with any meat or vegetarian dish in a tomato sauce.

NOTES

Frescobaldi 'Castiglioni' Chianti 2006

★ ★ ★ ½

DOCG CHIANTI $14.85   (545319)

Chianti, which is undoubtedly Italy's best-known wine region, turns out vast quantities of wine in a wide range of quality and prices. This one is simply well made and expresses all the character of the area. It's medium bodied, has concentrated and reasonably complex fruit flavours, and is balanced towards refreshing tanginess. This is an easy choice for any tomato-based Italian dish.

NOTES

....

....

....

....

Frescobaldi 'Nipozzano' Chianti Rufina Riserva 2005

★ ★ ★ ★

DOCG CHIANTI RUFINA RISERVA $21.75   (107276)

The Chianti region is divided into a number of sub-regions, including Rufina. "Nipozzano" is a long-time favourite, and recent vintages keep up the tradition of quality. This delivers high-toned fruit flavours that have depth and breadth and are complemented by a refreshing texture that orients it towards food. Drink it with well-seasoned red meats, such as a braised lamb shank.

NOTES

....

....

....

....

Italia 'i' Montepulciano d'Abruzzo 2006

★ ★ ★ ½

DOC MONTEPULCIANO D'ABRUZZO $10.35   (35154)

Italy exports many well-made wines at surprisingly low prices. This one is described as "Italian style in a bottle," and I'd say that's pretty close. It has good, rich fruit flavours with the refreshing texture characteristic of Italian reds. Medium-bodied and dry, it's a natural for any tomato-based Italian dish, from pizza to lasagna.

NOTES

....

....

....

....

Lungarotti 'Rubesco' 2005

★ ★ ★ ½

DOC ROSSO DI TORGIANO $13.95   (41947)

Torgiano is a wine town par excellence, with the Lungarotti winery nearby.
There's a great wine museum and plenty of places for tasting and drinking.
This medium-bodied blend of Sangiovese and Canaiolo grape varieties has
attractive fruit flavours and a juicy texture. It's dry with very light tannins
and goes well with veal Parmesan or any pasta in a tomato sauce.

NOTES

....

....

....

....

....

Marchesi di Montecristo 'Nerello del Bastardo' 2002

★ ★ ★ ★

VINO DA TAVOLA $13.05   (588913)

This was one of *those* discoveries when it first arrived in the LCBO a few
years ago. It was classified Vino da Tavola, which is the lowest rung on
the Italian wine scale, but it offered real quality and value. It still does.
Medium-bodied and dry, dry, dry, it has quite big tannins and dense fruit
flavours. Serve it with steak or other red meat, cooked medium-rare at most.

NOTES

....

....

....

....

....

Masi 'Bonacosta' Valpolicella Classico 2006

★ ★ ★ ★

DOC VALPOLICELLA CLASSICO $15.45   (285585)

This very attractive blend of three grape varieties (Corvina, Rondinella,
and Molinara) native to Italy makes for a delicious wine. Taste it and
you'll discover vibrant fruit flavours that have breadth and depth. It's dry
and a bit more than medium bodied, and the natural acidity in the grapes
gives it a refreshing texture that makes you think of food. Like veal or
chicken with a spicy tomato sauce.

NOTES

....

....

....

★ ★ ★ ★ ½ **Masi 'Campofiorin' 2005**

IGT ROSSO DEL VERONESE $17.45   (155051)

Campofiorin is a stylish wine that's reliable year after year. It's made by adding freshly fermented wine to the grape skins that remain after the super-rich Amarone is made. This produces dense, intense flavours of complex ripe fruit. It's more-than-medium bodied, dry, with a tangy texture, and a real treat to drink. Pour alongside spicy pasta dishes with grated Parmesan cheese.

NOTES

....
....
....
....

★ ★ ★ ★ ½ **Masi 'Costasera' Amarone della Valpolicella Classico 2004**

DOC AMARONE DELLA VALPOLICELLA CLASSICO

$37.45   (317057)

Amarone is made from grapes that are allowed to dry on bamboo mats for a few months before being pressed. The drying process creates more concentrated flavours, as this wine shows. Its layers of ripe and mature fruit are dense and well focused, and it has an opulent texture. Dry, moderately tannic, and with a tangy texture, it's an excellent choice for rich red meat dishes and aged hard cheeses.

NOTES

....
....
....
....

★ ★ ★ ★ ½ **Masi 'Modello' 2006**

IGT VENEZIE $11.95   (564674)

Very good values are to be found at all price points, but it's much more interesting when you find one around $10. Here's a wine that delivers quite concentrated flavours, good structure, and a very attractive texture that's round and refreshing. It's dry and medium bodied with light tannins, and it goes very well with tomato-based pasta and grilled red meats.

NOTES

....
....
....
....

Masi 'Serego Alighieri' Possessioni Rosso 2005

★ ★ ★ ★

IGT ROSSO DEL VERONESE $15.95   (447326)

Masi is a well-known producer of quality wines (and well represented in this book), and this delicious red blend (mainly Corvina and Sangiovese grape varieties) shows the value it offers, too. This has concentrated and nicely nuanced flavours, and you'll find the texture attractive and juicy. Medium-bodied and dry, it's a natural candidate for Italian dishes, from vegetarian pizza to veal scaloppini.

NOTES

Mezzomondo Negroamaro Rosso 2006

★ ★ ★ ½

IGT SALENTO $8.40   (588962)

Salento is a region in southern Italy—in the heel of the boot, if you think of Italy that way—and Negroamaro is a widely planted variety there. This is a quite robust red, with intense flavours and a mouth-filling and smooth texture. It's dry and medium bodied, and it pairs very well with grilled red meats or hearty vegetarian meals with mushrooms.

NOTES

Montalto Nero d'Avola/Cabernet Sauvignon 2006

★ ★ ★ ★ ½

IGT SICILIA $9.70   (621151)

For a long time, Sicily was better known for white wine than red, but in the last few years the reds, led by the native Nero d'Avola variety, have been going gangbusters. That local grape is most of the blend here, and it delivers rich, complex flavours of dark fruit and spice. It's almost full bodied, with a generous and tangy texture. This is pretty big and needs the same kind of food, so pair it with well-seasoned red meat.

NOTES

Negrar Amarone della Valpolicella Classico 2004
★ ★ ★ ★ ½
DOC AMARONE DELLA VALPOLICELLA CLASSICO

$32.75 (44784)

Plush, mouth-filling, and richly textured, this is a lovely Amarone that delivers firm tannins and layers of concentrated flavour. It has just the right acidity needed to contain the richness of the fruit and make a wine that pairs successfully with food. Enjoy this with any meal that features well-seasoned red meats. Alternatively, drink it with aged hard cheese, such as Parmigiano-Reggiano.

NOTES

Negrar 'Le Roselle' Ripasso Valpolicella Classico Superiore 2006
★ ★ ★ ★
DOC RIPASSO VALPOLICELLA CLASSICO SUPERIORE

$15.85 (620831)

Valpolicella is one of Italy's best-known wines. From a region in the northeast of the country, the wine can be a blend of up to seven different varieties. This is a good example, with well-defined and quite concentrated flavours that are bright and vibrant. There's substantial weight in the texture, but it's also refreshing. Medium-bodied and dry, it's a natural to open if you're eating pasta or a meat dish with a tomato-based sauce.

NOTES

Pasqua Merlot 2006
★ ★ ★
IGT VENEZIE

$13.90 (611780)

[1.5 Litres] Sometimes you need a lot a wine at a low price. It might be a party, a barbecue—some gathering where you need a decent, not-too-pricey red that will please a crowd and go with what you're eating. Try this one, a well-made Merlot that has enough of everything and not too much of anything. It's dry, full of flavour, and balanced, and teams well with red meat, chicken, pork, burgers, pizza, whatever.

NOTES

Rocca delle Macie Chianti Classico 2004

★ ★ ★ ½

DOCG CHIANTI CLASSICO $18.95   (741769)

[Vintages Essential] This is a long-time favourite *Chianti Classico*—the "Classico" meaning the grapes came from the original Chianti region, which has since been expanded. It's a quite classic young Chianti, with bright and vibrant flavours and a lively texture. Dry and medium-bodied, it goes well with Italian tomato-based dishes, whether pasta, meat, or pizza.

NOTES

....

....

....

....

....

Rocca delle Macie 'Vernaiolo' Chianti 2006

★ ★ ★ ★

DOCG CHIANTI $12.75   (269589)

The Chianti wine region produces tens of millions of bottles of wine a year, some of it exquisite, some of it not. If you are old enough to have been drinking in the '60s and '70s, you'll remember the not-so-exquisite Chiantis in wicker baskets. Vernaiolo is a stylish version with elegant and dense flavours of ripe fruit. It's dry and moderately tannic, juicy textured, and perfect with chicken Parmesan.

NOTES

....

....

....

....

....

Ruffino 'Il Ducale' 2005

★ ★ ★ ★

IGT TOSCANA $19.80   (27797)

"Il Ducale" is a compelling blend that's mainly Sangiovese (80 percent), then Merlot, with small contributions from other varieties. It's dry and medium bodied, and delivers a mouthful of tangy vibrant flavours that are consistent from attack (when it enters your mouth) to finish. The Sangiovese contributes good acidity, and the refreshing texture of the wine makes it a natural for dishes in a tomato-based sauce.

NOTES

....

....

....

★ ★ ★ ★ ½

Ruffino 'Riserva Ducale' Chianti Classico 2005

DOCG CHIANTI CLASSICO $25.75   (45195)

Chianti Classico is made from grapes grown in the original region of Chianti, often considered the premium-quality region. What you get here is certainly top-notch: a rich, opulent mouthful of intense and many layered flavours that are delivered on a full and tangy texture. It's dry and moderately tannic and goes wonderfully with pasta in a rich tomato-based sauce.

NOTES

....

....

....

....

★ ★ ★ ½

Straccali Chianti Classico 2006

DOCG CHIANTI $15.45   (19695)

Chianti is probably Italy's best-known wine region, even though many other areas (especially in southern Italy) are now producing good-value wines for the world market. This Chianti Classico (from the original Chianti region) delivers layered flavours with light tanginess. It's medium bodied and has drying tannins, and goes well with richly flavoured pizza or osso bucco.

NOTES

....

....

....

....

★ ★ ★ ★ ★

Tedeschi Amarone della Valpolicella Classico 2003

DOC AMARONE DELLA VALPOLICELLA CLASSICO

$44.95   (433417)

[Vintages Essential] The grapes for this wine are dried for four months during which they shrivel and the water in them evaporates, so they have more concentrated flavours when they're finally pressed. The wine is then aged two to three years in oak barrels and another six months in the bottle. Taste the process in its rich, intense, complex flavours and almost decadently opulent texture. It needs big, rich food, such as lamb, steak, or game.

NOTES

....

....

....

....

★ ★ ★ ½

Tedeschi 'Capitel dei Nicalo' Valpolicella Classico Superiore 2005

DOC VALPOLICELLA CLASSICO SUPERIORE $16.95   (984997)

This wine was made from grapes that have been allowed to dry for 30 days so they shrivel and lose water before being pressed. The resulting more-concentrated flavours come through loud and clear in the wine. It's well flavoured and has a fairly rich, dry, and tangy texture. Medium-weight, this is a good wine to open when you're serving meat in a tomato-based sauce.

NOTES

....

....

....

★ ★ ★ ★ ½

Terra d'Aligi Montepulciano d'Abruzzo 2005

DOC MONTEPULCIANO D'ABRUZZO $11.85   (28530)

This is a delicious Montepulciano, full of ripe fruit flavours that are concentrated, layered with complexity, and lifted by a lovely acidity that tilts it towards food. The texture is bright and refreshing, yet substantial and satisfying. It's medium bodied, dry, and lightly tannic, and a terrific choice for a wide range of meat-based Italian dishes.

NOTES

....

....

....

....

....

★ ★ ★ ★

Velletri 'Terre dei Volsci' Riserva 2003

DOC VELLETRI $13.95   (175141)

No, that *is* a weirdly shaped bottle. It's not the aftershock of the 16-percent-alcohol Zinfandel you drank last night. Velletri is a region in Lazio, south of Tuscany, and the reds from there are mostly Montepulciano and Sangiovese. This delivers a lovely smooth and tangy texture (sounds odd, but try it) with vibrant and focused flavours. Dry and medium-bodied, it's excellent with rich tomato-based pastas and pizzas.

NOTES

....

....

....

....

....

Villa Antinori 2005
★ ★ ★ ★

IGT TOSCANA $24.90   (53876)

The Antinori name is one of the best known in Tuscany, and the company produces quality wine from the highest level to more modest price points. This one has been a popular item for years. It offers lovely, layered flavours that are concentrated and complex, and a texture that's smooth and balanced. It's medium bodied, dry, and lightly tannic, and a great choice for osso bucco or veal in a rich tomato-based sauce.

NOTES

Vitae Sangiovese 2006
★ ★ ★ ½

IGT PUGLIA $10.85   (621029)

The Puglia region in the south of Italy produces vast amounts of wine made from many different varieties, including Sangiovese, which has migrated from further north. The wine in this distinctive bottle (a bonus for your table) is very well made and quite typical of the grape variety, with clean, crisp fruit flavours. Dry and medium-bodied, it's excellent with any tomato-based Italian dish.

NOTES

Zenato 'Ripassa' Valpolicella Superiore 2005
★ ★ ★ ★ ½

DOC VALPOLICELLA SUPERIORE $24.95   (479766)

[Vintages Essential] This is produced by adding the grape skins left over from making Amarone wine to Valpolicella so as to start a second fermentation. The Amarone skins (from dried grapes) add depth and complexity, making this wine especially robust and dense, with intense, complex flavours. It's full bodied, dry, and quite tannic, has a mouth-filling, generous texture, and is delicious with well-seasoned red meats or aged cheeses.

NOTES

NEW ZEALAND

NEW ZEALAND IS BEST KNOWN for its white wines, especially Sauvignon Blancs from the Marlborough region in the South Island. But it turns out many very good red wines, too, including Merlot and Cabernet from the North Island. The Pinot Noirs are especially impressive, but most are made in too-small volumes for the LCBO list.

Roy's Hill Cabernet/Merlot 2005

★ ★ ★ ★

HAWKES BAY $15.85   (024760)

Hawkes Bay, on the east coast of New Zealand's North Island, is an increasingly important wine region, and it's gaining a reputation for red wines, especially Merlot. This blend has well-defined fruit flavours with a fair measure of complexity. It's medium bodied, dry, and lightly tannic, and goes well with steak and roast beef.

NOTES

....

....

....

....

....

Sally Cat Pinot Noir 2006

★ ★ ★ ½

NEW ZEALAND $15.00   (610667)

This is another in the feline series by Coopers Creek. To stress the point, part of the profit from the sale of these wines goes to the Ontario SPCA. Purr-fect! This Pinot Noir captures much of the character of the best New Zealand Pinot, with ripe and vibrant fruit flavours and some complexity. It's medium bodied and dry, with light tannins, and goes well with portobello burgers or lamb.

NOTES

....

....

....

....

....

ONTARIO

ONTARIO PRODUCES A WIDE RANGE of red wines. The most successful varieties, of course, are those that thrive and ripen on a regular basis in its cool climate. They include Pinot Noir, Cabernet Franc, and Gamay. The best known of Ontario's four wine regions is Niagara Peninsula (which is now divided into a number of sub-regions). Lake Erie North Shore, which is somewhat warmer, is also represented in this list.

Wine labelled VQA (Vintners Quality Alliance), followed by a region, is made from grapes grown in that region. The VQA classification also means that the wine has been tested and tasted for quality. VQA wines from Ontario can be made only from grapes grown in Ontario. For a quality Ontario wine, look for the VQA symbol.

Most non-VQA wines in the Canada and Ontario sections of the LCBO are "Cellared in Canada" wines, which are blends of a small proportion of Ontario wine and a high percentage of foreign wine. Cellared in Canada wines are not included in this book because the range varies greatly from year to year, according to the Ontario grape harvest.

Birchwood Estate Cabernet Sauvignon 2005

★ ★ ★ ½

VQA NIAGARA PENINSULA $12.95   (26781)

Birchwood Estate is a small winery near the shore of Lake Ontario. This Cabernet Sauvignon shows good character in its quite concentrated flavours and the medium-weight, tangy, and refreshing texture. This is a dry red, with quite firm tannins. You might want to tame them by drinking this with red meat grilled no more than medium-rare or with aged cheddar.

NOTES

Cave Spring Cellars Cabernet/Merlot 2005

★ ★ ★ ★

VQA NIAGARA ESCARPMENT $16.05   (407270)

Here's a Niagara Cab-Merlot that has a lot going for it. The flavours are nicely concentrated and focused, and have good complexity. They're ripe with an ever-so-slight layer of underripeness that I think is very attractive. This is dry and medium bodied, with a firm texture, and drying tannins. It makes a very good partner for grilled red meats or for well-flavoured chicken dishes, like coq au vin.

NOTES

Cave Spring Cellars Gamay 2006

★ ★ ★ ★

VQA NIAGARA PENINSULA $13.05   (228569)

Gamay grapes grow successfully in the Niagara Peninsula, but it's a variety overlooked by many wine drinkers. This one from Cave Spring is lovely. It has bright flavours of fresh fruit, and a refreshing texture. It's dry and light- to medium-bodied, and the juiciness in the texture makes you think of food. Serve it slightly chilled with roast chicken or baked ham.

NOTES

★ ★ ★ ★ **Château des Charmes 'Estate Bottled'**
Cabernet/Merlot 2004

VQA NIAGARA-ON-THE-LAKE $19.95   (222372)

[Vintages Essential] The founder of Château des Charmes, Paul Bosc Sr., is one of the pioneers of Niagara's modern wine industry and was awarded the Order of Canada for his role in developing it. This is a well-made, cool-climate blend that delivers good structure, clearly defined fruit flavours, and a solid and refreshing texture. It's just the wine for a thick slice of rare or medium-rare roast beef. (Note that this bottle has a black label.)

NOTES

★ ★ ★ ½ **Château des Charmes Gamay Noir 2006**

VQA NIAGARA PENINSULA $12.45   (57349)

Gamay is the grape variety used to make Beaujolais, but this wine is more substantial than most generic Beaujolais. What you get are quite concentrated flavours and a fairly generous texture that's enlivened by a dose of food-friendly acidity. It's just medium bodied and leaves an astringent feeling in your mouth. This will go well with roast turkey and cranberries, and a wide range of salads, especially salade Niçoise.

NOTES

★ ★ ★ ★ **Château des Charmes Gamay Noir 'Droit' 2006**

VQA NIAGARA PENINSULA $16.95   (582353)

This lovely wine is made from a clone of the Gamay variety discovered in the vineyards of Château des Charmes by its founder, Paul Bosc Sr. The vine's shoots grow straight up (*droit*) and it's now a registered variety. The wine is all rich, dense flavours with great tanginess. Dry and medium-bodied, it goes well with red meats or with grilled spicy sausages.

NOTES

Château des Charmes Pinot Noir 2006

★ ★ ★ ½

VQA NIAGARA PENINSULA $14.45   (195511)

This is Pinot Noir in a lighter style (and lighter colour) but it has good character—not to mention good pedigree, coming, as it does, from one of Ontario's high-performing wineries. Look for lively and high-toned flavours and a bright texture. It's medium bodied and dry, and it goes well with salmon grilled on a cedar plank.

NOTES

....
....
....
....
....
....

Colio Cabernet/Merlot 2006

★ ★ ★ ★

VQA LAKE ERIE NORTH SHORE $11.95   (432054)

Colio wines are made from grapes grown in one of Ontario's most southerly and warmer regions. This Cabernet/Merlot blend has concentrated and dense flavours of ripe fruit. It's fairly dry and medium bodied, with light tannins. The fruit's richness makes this a good wine to serve with grilled red meat, like steak or lamb, but it also goes well with burgers, or with pizza heavy on meat and mushrooms.

NOTES

....
....
....
....

EastDell Black Cab 2006

★ ★ ★

VQA NIAGARA PENINSULA $12.95   (609875)

This wine's name makes me think of a London taxi—except that the wine comes at a reasonable price. You get a tangy mouthful of complex flavours, with some added spiciness. A blend of several varieties, including Cabernet Sauvignon and Baco Noir, it's medium bodied and lightly tannic. It goes well with hearty vegetarian dishes featuring wild mushrooms.

NOTES

....
....
....
....

EastDell Cabernet/Merlot 2006
★ ★ ★
VQA NIAGARA PENINSULA $12.95   (620187)

This is a cool-climate Cab-Merlot, so look for good structure and refreshing acidity. Don't expect the big, upfront blends such as you might get from Australia. The flavours here are solid with a little complexity, and the wine is tangy and refreshing in your mouth. It's very dry with prominent tannins, and it goes well with a grilled veal chop or with red meats.

NOTES

....

....

....

....

Henry of Pelham Baco Noir 2006
★ ★ ★ ★
VQA ONTARIO $13.75   (270926)

A few wineries make successful wine from Baco Noir, a variety that's widely grown in Niagara. It can taste a bit unusual (it's sometimes described as "funky"), but it has a real following. Henry of Pelham is known as a key producer. Look for rich, pungent flavours, with a lot of complexity. Dry, medium-bodied, and nicely balanced, it pairs happily with rich, well-seasoned red meat and game. This wine is also available in a half-bottle size (375 mL) for $6.95 (598938).

NOTES

....

....

....

....

Henry of Pelham Cabernet Franc 2006
★ ★ ★ ★
VQA NIAGARA PENINSULA $14.25   (27839)

Since it ripens earlier than many other red grape varieties, Cabernet Franc is well-suited to Niagara's cool climate. You'll find this wine has ripe and quite complex fruit flavours, with characteristic hints of greenness, and a fairly rich and tangy texture. The tannins are still forward, and you might want to rein them in with rare or medium-rare red meat or aged cheese.

NOTES

....

....

....

....

Henry of Pelham Gamay 2006

★ ★ ★ ½

VQA SHORTHILLS BENCH $13.90   (291112)

[Vintages Essential] Shorthills Bench is a sub-region of the Niagara Peninsula and the location of this winery. Gamay grows well in Niagara, and this one from Henry of Pelham shows good character in the bright, focused fruit and the sleek, refreshing texture. It's dry, just medium bodied, and it goes well with roast chicken or roast turkey and cranberries.

NOTES

....

....

....

....

Henry of Pelham 'Meritage' Cabernet/Merlot 2005

★ ★ ★ ½

VQA NIAGARA PENINSULA $15.25   (504241)

Meritage is a name used quite widely in North America to denote blends of the main Bordeaux grapes (for reds these are Cabernet Sauvignon, Merlot, and Cabernet Franc). It's pronounced to rhyme with "heritage." This blend is a lighter-style red, with quite well-defined flavours, moderate tannins, and a clean, dry texture that's refreshing and friendly to food. Drink this with roast or grilled chicken or pork, or a grilled veal chop.

NOTES

....

....

....

....

....

Henry of Pelham Pinot Noir 2006

★ ★ ★

VQA NIAGARA PENINSULA $17.25   (013904)

Henry of Pelham is one of Niagara's mid-size quality wineries, run by the friendly Speck brothers (three of them). With good balance between the fruit and acidity, this Pinot Noir makes a successful partner for grilled lamb, veal chops, or well-herbed roast chicken. It's medium bodied, with attractive and vibrant flavours and a lively, refreshing, and well-balanced texture.

NOTES

....

....

....

....

....

Henry of Pelham Reserve Baco Noir 2005
★ ★ ★ ★

VQA ONTARIO $24.95   (461699)

[Vintages Essential] Baco Noir is a cross between Folle Blanche, a French
grape variety, and another whose identity is uncertain. It used to be grown
in various parts of France (including Burgundy). In this Reserve level,
Henry of Pelham have produced a wonderfully rich and soft-textured
wine, with unmistakable and complex Baco flavours. It's finely balanced
and a great wine to serve with well-seasoned, grilled red meats.

NOTES
....
....
....
....

Hillebrand 'Artist Series' Meritage 2005
★ ★ ★ ★ ½

VQA NIAGARA PENINSULA $12.95   (56390)

Meritage (rhymes with "heritage") is a name developed to refer to blends of
grapes allowed in Bordeaux wine. They used to be called "Bordeaux blends"
but "Bordeaux" is now used only to refer to that region. So this is a blend
of Cabernets Sauvignon and Franc, as well as Merlot. It's got great flavour
(complex and rich), a full and tangy texture, and good structure. Dry and
quite tannic, it's a natural for red meats cooked no more than medium.

NOTES
....
....
....
....

Jackson-Triggs 'Proprietors' Reserve' Meritage 2006
★ ★ ★ ★

VQA NIAGARA PENINSULA $13.25   (526228)

The word "Meritage" was devised to describe a blend of Bordeaux grapes
when the name "Bordeaux" was restricted to wines from that region in
France. This brings together Merlot, Cabernet Sauvignon, and Cabernet
Franc (in that order) in an attractive red with concentrated fruit character
and a mouth-filling and nicely balanced texture. It's dry and quite tannic
and goes well with grilled red meats.

NOTES
....
....
....
....

Mike Weir Cabernet/Merlot 2006

★ ★ ★ ★

VQA NIAGARA PENINSULA $18.80   (109)

Mike Weir has compelling initials in the world of wine: MW stands for Master of Wine, the highest qualification in the field. He's also made a pretty compelling red here. It delivers solid flavours that display a little greenness (what's a golfer without a green?) and a fairly robust texture. It's medium weight, dry, and has firm tannins, and it pairs very well with grilled red meats.

NOTES
....
....
....
....

Pelee Island Cabernet/Merlot Reserve 2006

★ ★ ★ ½

VQA ONTARIO $14.85   (435321)

Pelee Island Winery's labels celebrate the rich variety of wildlife on the island and the winery is active in many conservation projects. This classic blend delivers intense and rich flavours with some complexity and a seam of fruit sweetness at the core. The texture is soft and it's properly balanced. Medium-bodied and dry, it goes well with red meats and with hearty meat-based pasta dishes.

NOTES
....
....
....
....

Pelee Island Pinot Noir Reserve 2006

★ ★ ★ ½

VQA PELEE ISLAND $14.95   (458521)

Pelee Island, in Lake Erie, is Canada's most southerly point and Ontario's warmest wine region. There are vineyards on the island, but Pelee Island Winery's facilities are on the mainland. This Pinot Noir is medium bodied and dry, with light tannins. The flavours are solid and complex and it's full and tangy to the taste. This is a fairly dense wine that can be lightened by 10 to 15 minutes in the fridge. Serve it with grilled veal or lamb chops.

NOTES
....
....
....
....

Peller 'Heritage Series' Cabernet Franc 2006

★ ★ ★ ½

VQA NIAGARA PENINSULA $11.75   (582833)

Cabernet Franc's benchmark regions (those that produce classic styles of it) are Bordeaux and the Loire Valley in France. It also does very well in Niagara's cool growing conditions, and this inexpensive example has all the characteristics you should expect. The flavours are well defined but not too assertive, and quite complex. It's dry and lightly tannic, and the texture is taut and refreshing. Drink this with lamb or veal chops.

NOTES

....

....

....

....

Reif Estate Cabernet/Merlot 2006

★ ★ ★ ½

VQA NIAGARA PENINSULA $14.05   (565713)

Cabernet Sauvignon and Merlot first met in Bordeaux. Whether it was love at first sight, no one knows, but they've been renewing their vows at every opportunity. On this occasion they've produced a nice cool-climate version, with quite concentrated and well-defined flavours and a texture that's fairly generous and crisp. Dry and medium-bodied, it has firm tannins and is a good choice for grilled red meats or generously seasoned chicken.

NOTES

....

....

....

....

Stoney Ridge Reserve Pinot Noir 2006

★ ★ ★ ½

VQA ONTARIO $17.15   (669291)

The 2006 vintage was not stellar for Pinot Noir in the Niagara Peninsula, but this one has good character. Although the colour is quite good, this is Pinot in a lighter style. There's fruitiness, with some pretty nuances, and the texture is vibrant and refreshing. It's dry, light- to medium-bodied, and it goes well with roast chicken or with turkey and cranberry sauce.

NOTES

....

....

....

....

Trius Cabernet Franc 2004

★ ★ ★ ★

VQA NIAGARA PENINSULA $14.95   (587964)

The Trius line from Hillebrand Estates is very good across the board and this medium-bodied Cabernet Franc fits effortlessly into the range. It's quite stylish, with concentrated flavours of ripe fruit, and the merest hint of greenness that's a hallmark of many Cab Francs. It's dry, with firm tannins, and is a great choice for full-flavoured red meat, or meat or vegetarian stews.

NOTES

....

....

....

....

Trius Cabernet Sauvignon 2006

★ ★ ★ ★

VQA NIAGARA PENINSULA $14.95   (587956)

Trius was originally a blend of three Bordeaux grape varieties, but it was so successful that the winery launched individual varieties under the Trius name. This Cabernet is very well made and delivers flavours that are deep, broad, and complex. The texture is smooth and quite generous, and dry with moderate tannins. It's medium bodied and goes well with red meats or juicy hamburgers.

NOTES

....

....

....

....

Trius Merlot 2006

★ ★ ★ ★

VQA NIAGARA PENINSULA $14.95   (587907)

The Trius line really is one of Niagara's big success stories: consistent quality at a good price, such that Hillebrand (the producer) added "Trius" in large letters to its roadside signage. This is a lovely soft Merlot that delivers well-defined and complex flavours and a fairly dense but balanced texture. It's dry with moderate tannins, and goes well with grilled or roasted red meat.

NOTES

....

....

....

....

Trius Red 2006

★ ★ ★ ★ ½

VQA NIAGARA PENINSULA $19.95   (303800)

[Vintages Essential] Trius Red has been a quality wine for as long it's been produced. A blend of Cabernet Sauvignon, Cabernet Franc, and Merlot, it's aged in oak barrels for a year. It is quite delicious, with concentrated and defined flavours, and a smooth, fairly generous texture. Medium-bodied and dry, with moderate tannins, it's a natural for red meats or herbed roast chicken.

NOTES

....
....
....
....
....

Wayne Gretzky 'No. 99' Merlot 2006

★ ★ ★

VQA NIAGARA PENINSULA $15.95   (63966)

Don't you wonder how much input celebrities like Wayne Gretzky have in the wines named after them? Is this served at dinner parties at the Gretzky house? No reason why not, as it's a decent Merlot with solid, straightforward flavours, and a tangy, well-balanced, and moderately tannic texture. Dry and medium-bodied, it goes nicely with simply prepared grilled red meats or generously herbed roast chicken.

NOTES

....
....
....
....
....

OREGON

OREGON HAS ESTABLISHED A REPUTATION for Pinot Noir, especially from the cool growing conditions of the Willamette Valley. Unfortunately, few of them are included in the LCBO's listings.

Amity Pinot Noir 2006

★ ★ ★ ★

WILLAMETTE VALLEY $29.70   (124594)

This Pinot Noir performs well, year after year. It marks a nice contrast to many New World Pinot Noirs, in which fruit overpowers everything else. This is a kind of midpoint effort, nicely located between Burgundy and Jammyland. What you get here is lovely rich, textured fruit and a remarkably light and refreshing texture. It's medium bodied, bone dry, and goes very well with grilled salmon.

NOTES

....

....

....

....

....

PORTUGAL

PORTUGAL IS BEST KNOWN FOR PORT, and it seems logical that some of its best red wines are made from grape varieties permitted in port. They tend to be full of flavour, assertive in texture, and big bodied. This also means that Portuguese reds are mainly made from indigenous grape varieties, and producers have generally resisted planting the so-called "international varieties," such as Cabernet Sauvignon and Syrah.

The name of a region following "DOC" (*Denominação de Origem Controlada*) signifies a designated Portuguese wine region.

Aliança Foral Reserva 2006

★ ★ ★ ★

DOC DOURO $8.10   (239046)

The Douro Valley is best known for port, but we're seeing more and more table wines from there, too. This blend of several grape varieties delivers dense, concentrated flavours with a lot of complexity. It's medium bodied, very dry, with upfront tannins. It goes best with aged cheddar or red meat cooked no more than medium-rare.

NOTES

Aveleda 'Charamba' 2005

★ ★ ★ ½

DOC DOURO $8.95   (352963)

Sometimes you wonder how it's possible to buy land, plant vines, wait while they mature, manage them, harvest the grapes, make wine, bottle it, ship it, market it, sell it, pay everyone who handles it, and still sell it for under $10. This blend is quite gutsy, with a rustic, tangy texture, and quite intense flavours. It's dry and juicy, and goes well with burgers, pizza, and red meats.

NOTES

Duque de Viseu 2005

★ ★ ★ ★

DOC DÃO $12.85   (546309)

[Vintages Essential] The Dão wine region has long been known for its bold reds, and this is a good example. It's made from Touriga Nacional (one of the major grape varieties in port) and Tinta Roriz (known across the border in Spain as Tempranillo), which give it concentrated flavours with some complexity. Dry, quite tannic, and medium-bodied, it goes well with grilled red meats.

NOTES

Pedras do Monte Castelão 2005

★ ★ ★ ½

VINHO REGIONAL TERRAS DO SADO $10.10   (565762)

Castelão is a grape variety indigenous to southern Portugal, where it's also known as *Periquita* and by several other names. As this example shows, it can make a not-too-complicated, fruity wine with a refreshing, juicy texture. It's dry, light- to medium-bodied, has good flavour, and goes well with dishes like herbed roast chicken and tomato-based pasta.

NOTES
....
....
....
....
....

Terra Boa 'Old Vines' 2006

★ ★ ★

VINHO REGIONAL TRANSMONTANO $7.95   (590364)

Made from old plantings of indigenous grapes, this is a well-priced red that's ideal for a wide range of food. It's great for barbecues (especially when there's a crowd), and it goes nicely with hearty stews, whether meat or vegetarian. The wine is very dry, with fairly prominent tannins, has concentrated, ripe flavours, and a lively and quite refreshing texture.

NOTES
....
....
....
....
....

Vila Regia Reserva 2005

★ ★ ★ ½

DOC DOURO $11.85   (613950)

This is produced from four of the scores of grape varieties that can be used for making port. It has the characteristic features of red wines from the Douro region (where port comes from): intense flavours, substantial weight, good structure, a mouth-filling texture, and drying tannins. It goes well with hearty dishes, so pair it with a winter stew or barbecued red meats.

NOTES
....
....
....
....

Vinha do Monte 2005

★ ★ ★

VINHO REGIONAL ALENTEJANO $9.90   (621813)

From the plains of southern Portugal comes this medium- to full-bodied red that's astringently dry. The tannins are quite prominent, but you can deal with them by drinking this with aged hard cheese (such as cheddar) or red meat cooked no more than medium-rare. Under the tannins, the flavours are concentrated and solid, and the texture is appealingly tangy.

NOTES

....

....

....

....

Vista Touriga Nacional 2005

★ ★ ★ ½

VINHO REGIONAL BEIRAS $13.10   (613919)

Beiras is a region in north-central Portugal, where international grape varieties, like Chardonnay and Cabernet Sauvignon, can be used. But this wine is made from the country's most important indigenous grape, Touriga Nacional. It's astringently dry, with attractive deep flavours, and has firm tannins. Medium-bodied and quite tangy textured, it goes well with burgers and spicy sausages.

NOTES

....

....

....

....

SOUTH AFRICA

MOST OF THE WINE REGIONS OF SOUTH AFRICA are warm, and this tends to make for reds that have concentrated flavours and fairly high alcohol. The conditions are right for a wide range of grape varieties. The country's signature red grape is Pinotage, a cross of two varieties that was developed there in the 1920s. More popular varieties found in the LCBO are Shiraz, Merlot, and Cabernet Sauvignon.

Wines from official South African wine regions are called "Wines of Origin." In this list, the letters "WO" followed by a region indicate where the wine is from.

Bellingham Shiraz/Viognier 2005

★ ★ ★ ★ ½
WO WESTERN REGION $13.85   (554360)

For years, Bellingham made a terrific Shiraz in a fruity New World style.
But starting with the 2005 vintage, the winery altered its stylistic course
and came up with this really attractive and elegant Shiraz with "a dash of
Viognier" (actually, 2 percent). This is in a Rhône style, with more structure and restraint but no loss of concentration of flavour. The texture is
wonderful, and this is great with red meats.

NOTES
....
....
....
....

Cathedral Cellar Cabernet Sauvignon 2004

★ ★ ★ ★
WO COASTAL REGION $17.75   (328567)

[Vintages Essential] This is a lovely Cabernet that manages to combine
easy drinking appeal with a decent level of complexity. The flavours are
concentrated and layered, rich and yet nicely restrained, and it's a very
pleasant experience. The texture is light on its feet but still substantial.
Medium-bodied and dry, with modest tannic grip, this is a red you can
drink on its own, but it's also good with a grilled veal chop.

NOTES
....
....
....
....

Durbanville Hills Shiraz 2005

★ ★ ★
WO DURBANVILLE $13.05   (22269)

Although Australians grabbed Shiraz as their signature wine and made it
the big variety success story of the 1990s, they don't have the field entirely
to themselves. South Africa produces some notable examples. This one is
well made and delivers good fruitiness. Not too complex but flavoursome,
it teams happily with burgers and red meat.

NOTES
....
....
....
....

★ ★ ★ ★ **Fairview 'Goats Do Roam' 2005**

WO WESTERN CAPE $12.95 (718940)

[Vintages Essential] The story goes that the Fairview goats got into the vineyards and ate the best and tastiest fruit. (Who can deny the goats have a great future as vine consultants?) It's also a play on words for the Côtes du Rhône grape varieties used in this blend. Consistently well made, vintage after vintage, this wine represents good value. Look for luscious fruit flavours here, and drink it with barbecued red meats.

NOTES

★ ★ ★ ½ **Kumala Merlot/Pinotage 2007**

WO WESTERN CAPE $9.80 (572610)

Pinotage is South Africa's signature grape variety, a hybrid developed there in the 1920s. In this blend, it works with Merlot to give colour, flavour density, and some complexity. You end up with a fruity red with some pungency. It's dry, medium bodied, and fairly simple, and has a slightly rustic texture, but it's well balanced and a great match for barbecued spare ribs and burgers.

NOTES

★ ★ ★ ★ **Nederburg Cabernet Sauvignon 2006**

WO WESTERN CAPE $12.75 (111526)

The Nederburg brand dates back two centuries and is one of South Africa's most recognizable names in wine. This Cabernet shows that you can produce big volumes (over a million cases a year) and still maintain quality. It's dry and medium bodied, and has quite rich flavours and a vibrant, refreshing texture that makes it ideal for food. Drink it with grilled steak.

NOTES

Nederburg Shiraz 2006

★ ★ ★ ★

WO WESTERN CAPE $12.85   (527457)

This is a rather plush Shiraz with rich and complex flavours that ride in on a much more refreshing texture than many Shirazes at this price. The fruit flavours are ripe, concentrated, and nicely sculpted and the texture is generous and smooth. You'll find it's easy-drinking and an excellent choice for well-seasoned grilled red meats or barbecued ribs.

NOTES

....

....

....

....

....

Obikwa Cabernet Sauvignon 2007

★ ★ ★

WO WESTERN CAPE $9.50   (665323)

Obikwa takes its name from one of the earliest peoples that inhabited the Cape region of South Africa. Open a bottle of this Cabernet and you'll get pretty intense aromas and flavours—nothing very complex, but certainly attractive. The texture is tangy and refreshing, and it's dry, medium bodied, and very slightly tannic. There's a lot to like here, especially when you drink it with pizza, burgers, or ribs.

NOTES

....

....

....

....

Railroad Red Shiraz/Cabernet 2005

★ ★ ★ ½

WO WESTERN CAPE $12.20   (665273)

This wine is produced by the Graham Beck winery. Beck was involved in many industries, including rail transportation, before he got into wine, and he's been successful in all. This medium-bodied Shiraz/Cabernet blend is an easy-drinking red that's got the intensity of Shiraz with the structure of Cabernet. Look for well-concentrated flavours, light tannins, and a juicy texture. Drink it with chicken, pizza, and burgers.

NOTES

....

....

....

....

★ ★ ★ ½ **Robertson Winery Shiraz 2007**

WO ROBERTSON $11.95 (610949)

Robertson is one of South Africa's smaller designated wine regions that produce WO (Wines of Origin) wines. This is a straightforward, solid, well-made Shiraz that delivers concentrated ripe flavours with a fruit-sweet core, all on a fairly generous and tangy platform. It's a bit more than medium-bodied, and it goes nicely with red meats, especially if they're well seasoned or spicy.

NOTES

★ ★ ★ **Robert's Rock Cabernet Sauvignon/Merlot 2006**

WO WESTERN CAPE $8.95 (544668)

This is a straightforward wine. It's not complex, it's not demanding, but it has good solid flavours and a texture that's clean and refreshing. Medium-bodied and dry, with light tannins, this would be an excellent choice of wine if you're serving fairly full-flavoured food to a crowd at a barbecue or other party.

NOTES

★ ★ ★ ★ **Roodeberg Red 2005**

WO WESTERN CAPE $13.00 (007187)

This is a consistently impressive wine from the huge KWV wine coopera-tive. It's a blend that's mainly Cabernet Sauvignon, and it delivers a solid attack of rich and intense flavours and a texture that's generous and tangy. Medium-bodied and very dry, with tannins you feel on your gums, it's a red you'll want to match up with well-seasoned grilled red meats.

NOTES

Two Oceans Shiraz 2007

★ ★ ★

WO WESTERN CAPE $10.15   (699249)

Two Oceans is named for the point off South Africa where the Atlantic and the Indian oceans meet. You'd think these wines would be blends. But this is a Shiraz, and it's good value at this price, flavour-filled without much complexity, and easygoing in texture. There's a little tanginess, some light tannins (it's a dry wine), and overall it delivers a very pleasant mouthful. Sip it alone or drink with pizza, roast chicken, or burgers.

NOTES

....

....

....

....

....

Tribal Merlot 2006

★ ★ ★ ½

WO COASTAL REGION $9.20   (623702)

Like most South African reds, produced in warm-climate conditions, this Merlot delivers intense, concentrated, ripe fruit flavours. Medium-bodied and dry, the wine has a solid and tangy texture and isn't too complicated. It's a good choice for everyday meals like hamburgers, meatloaf, or meaty pizzas.

NOTES

....

....

....

....

Ubuntu Shiraz 2006

★ ★ ★

WO WESTERN CAPE $9.95   (665281)

Ubuntu is a Zulu/Xhola word that means something like "having feelings of humanity and altruism towards others." Open a bottle with friends and you'll capture the spirit. You'll certainly enjoy the wine at this price. It delivers ripe fruit flavours and a little warmth in the mouth. Medium-bodied with a hint of fruit sweetness, it goes well with seasoned red meats.

NOTES

....

....

....

....

....

SPAIN

SPAIN IS BEST KNOWN FOR ITS RED WINES. Among the many regions, Rioja is probably the most recognizable, but you'll find reds from a number of others on this list. Tempranillo is Spain's signature grape variety, but wine is made from many other native and international varieties, as this selection shows.

Campo Viejo Rioja Reserva 2003

★ ★ ★ ★

DOC RIOJA $18.45   (137810)

A Rioja Reserva has to age in barrel and bottle for a longer period than a generic Rioja before going on sale. For that reason, Reservas tend to have more intensity and complexity. This one is typical. It delivers concentrated and complex flavours, a fairly rich and tangy texture, and good tannic structure. Medium-bodied and dry, it goes well with grilled or roast lamb.

NOTES

....

....

....

....

Castillo de Almansa Reserva 2004

★ ★ ★ ½

DO ALMANSA $11.85   (270363)

Almansa is a small wine region not far inland from Spain's Mediterranean coast, where the days get very hot during the growing season. It shows in this wine, which has concentrated flavours of sweet fruit with some spiciness. It's medium bodied and bone dry with firm tannins, and goes nicely with well-seasoned red meat dishes, including hearty winter stews.

NOTES

....

....

....

....

Conde de Valdemar Crianza Rioja 2004

★ ★ ★ ★

DOC RIOJA $14.45   (356089)

To qualify for "Crianza" status, a Rioja wine spends at least one year in a barrel and has time in the bottle before it can be released for sale in its third year. This example delivers on both flavour and texture. You'll find attractive, complex, and concentrated fruit, and a fairly compact texture with some tanginess. Medium-bodied, dry, and lightly tannic, it goes well with roasted red meats.

NOTES

....

....

....

....

....

Julián Chivite 'Gran Feudo' Reserva 2003

★ ★ ★ ½

DO NAVARRA $15.95   (479014)

[Vintages Essential] This is a blend of Tempranillo, Cabernet Sauvignon, and Merlot, giving an international spin to Spain's signature grape variety. The flavours are quite concentrated with reasonably good complexity, and they're well complemented by the tangy texture. Dry, medium-bodied, and moderately tannic, it pairs nicely with hearty winter stews, either meat-based or vegetarian.

NOTES

....

....

....

....

Mad Dogs and Englishmen 2006

★ ★ ★ ★

DO JUMILLA $14.05   (669135)

According to Noel Coward, only mad dogs and Englishmen go out in the midday sun. He might have been referring to the Jumilla wine region, where summer temperatures reach 40°C. Maybe that explains the intense and complex fruit flavours here. This Mourvèdre/Cabernet/Shiraz blend is dry and moderately tannic, and is a natural for well-seasoned red meats.

NOTES

....

....

....

....

....

Marqués de Riscal Reserva Rioja 2003

★ ★ ★ ★ ★

DOC RESERVA RIOJA $24.30   (032656)

This is one beautiful Rioja, a red from Spain's best-known wine region, which was, for many years, the only region awarded Spain's highest-quality classification (DOC). This wine is mainly Tempranillo, which is Rioja's main grape variety. Here, it's expressed in lovely, pungent, complex aromas and flavours, fine balance, and a dry and smooth texture with moderate tannins. Drink this with grilled rack of lamb.

NOTES

....

....

....

....

Los Molinos Gran Reserva 1999

★★★ ½

DO VALDEPEÑAS $15.00   (620971)

The designation "Gran Reserva" means that the wine is aged for years
before being put on the market. This is one of the oldest wines in the
LCBO's General Purchase list. It's very dry and has the flavours you often
get with older wines: less vibrant and somewhat faded fruit. But it's still
attractive and goes well with roast chicken and dishes with mushrooms.

NOTES

....

....

....

....

Montecillo Crianza Rioja 2004

★★★ ½

DOC RIOJA $14.95   (144493)

In Spanish wine law, a "Crianza" wine has to undergo aging in oak barrels as well as aging in bottles at the winery. In Rioja, that means at least
one year in oak plus two in the bottle before it goes on sale. This example
shows quite intense and somewhat complex flavours, and a texture that's
medium bodied and quite tangy. Drink it with a dish that features meat
in a tomato-based sauce.

NOTES

....

....

....

....

Montecillo Reserva Rioja 2002

★★★★

DOC RIOJA $19.00   (621003)

Reserva Riojas like this one are relatively old because to be labelled
"Reserva," the wines have to be aged in barrels, then bottled for at least
three years before they're released. Think of them as pre-cellared. This is
bone dry with firm tannins, and the flavours are ripe, layered, and complex. Medium- to full-bodied, it goes well with stuffed pork tenderloin.

NOTES

....

....

....

....

Osborne 'Dominio de Malpica' 2004

★ ★ ★ ★

VINO DE LA TIERRA DE CASTILLA $14.85   (32011)

This is a 100 percent Cabernet Sauvignon regional wine that's big, bold, and quite stylish. It's medium- to full-bodied, with a dry texture and upfront tannins. The flavours are concentrated and layered, with evidence of the oak aging, and it has a rich and tangy texture. You can drink this with a wide range of full-flavoured red meats or with cheeses like aged cheddar.

NOTES

Osborne 'Solaz' Tempranillo/Cabernet Sauvignon 2005

★ ★ ★

VINO DE LA TIERRA DE CASTILLA $10.45   (610188)

Osborne is an old (founded in the 18th century) Spanish winery and you'll see its bull logo on billboards (bullboards?) all over Spain. This straightforward blend of Spain's icon grape and Cabernet delivers nicely concentrated flavours and a tangy texture. It's dry and medium bodied, and it goes well with grilled red meats and any meat dish that's in a tomato-based sauce.

NOTES

Red Guitar Old Vine Tempranillo/Garnacha 2006

★ ★ ★ ½

DO NAVARRA $12.85   (54007)

With 007 in its product code, this ought to be a killer wine. In fact it's pretty good for the price, delivering bright fruit flavours with some complexity, and a refreshing and tangy texture. It's bone dry, medium bodied, and lightly tannic. Don't shake it or stir it. Just pour it when you're serving roast chicken, pasta, or meat dishes with a tomato-based sauce.

NOTES

Toro 2006

★ ★ ★ ★

DO TORO $13.40   (19570)

Toro is not only Spanish for "bull," but is also a Spanish wine region with a reputation for high quality. It's easy to be bullish about this wine at this price. You get really intense fruit flavours with decent complexity and a big, tangy texture with drying tannins. Don't fight this bull; pour it with well-seasoned red meats and rich stews.

NOTES

....

....

....

....

Torres 'Gran Coronas' Cabernet Sauvignon Riserva 2004

★ ★ ★ ★

DO PENEDÈS $18.95   (36483)

[Vintages Essential] Torres is one of the great names in Spanish wine, and this Cabernet Sauvignon (with a little Tempranillo blended in to give it some Spanish blood) shows the quality and value that underlie its reputation. The fruit is sweet, ripe, layered, and concentrated, and the texture is generous and tangy. It's medium-to-full in body and dry, and has a good tannic grip. Enjoy it with grilled red meats.

NOTES

....

....

....

....

....

WASHINGTON

WARM GROWING CONDITIONS IN THE SOUTH of Washington
State are excellent for red wine. The most important varieties are
Merlot and Cabernet Sauvignon.

Columbia Crest Cabernet Sauvignon 2005

★ ★ ★ ★

COLUMBIA VALLEY $14.80   (332320)

Columbia Crest, one of Washington's largest wineries, turns out a range of very good wines. Its strength is reds, and this medium-bodied Cabernet is a good example. It's very well made, and all the components are nicely aligned. The flavours show ripeness, not sweet jamminess, and the tannins contribute to the dryness without interfering with your enjoyment. Drink it with grilled red meats.

NOTES

....

....

....

....

....

THE ROSÉS

ROSÉS ARE TOO OFTEN CRITICIZED, even by supposedly wine-knowledgeable people, as being too sweet, too simple, and not worthy of serious attention. But although many of these wines are off-dry or sweet, they go very well with food for that reason. And most have good flavours and a refreshing texture. One question: Why aren't *all* these rosés sealed with screw caps?

Beringer White Zinfandel 2007

★ ★ ★ ½

CALIFORNIA $10.00   (239756)

The origins of modern white Zinfandel are a bit murky. When it was first made in the early 1970s, by the Sutter Home winery, it really was white. The rosé version followed soon after but, for some reason, the name wasn't changed. No matter, because everyone knows white is the new pink. This one has bright, sweet fruit flavours that are matched by a zippy, clean, and refreshing texture. Drink it alone or with spicy appetizers.

NOTES

....

....

....

Cave Spring Rosé 2007

★ ★ ★ ½

VQA NIAGARA PENINSULA $13.05   (295006)

Today many winemakers are trying to make "serious" rosés, and too many are reds in all but colour. Taste them blind and you'd think you were drinking red wine. This rosé, made mainly from Cabernet Sauvignon and Cabernet Franc, is in a lighter, more familiar style, with vibrant, fresh, fruity flavours. It's dry, with a crisp, clean texture, and goes well with roast ham or turkey, or summer salads.

NOTES

....

....

....

Fetzer 'Valley Oaks' White Zinfandel 2007

★ ★ ★ ½

CALIFORNIA $10.00   (517458)

Rosé wine was first made from Zinfandel way back in the 1800s, but it wasn't called "white" then. The modern, pink version began in the mid-1970s, and producers haven't looked back since. It's the second most popular style in the US, after Chardonnay. Fetzer's is deliciously sweet, with lively flavours and a bright texture. It's perfect for summer sipping or to match with spicy appetizers.

NOTES

....

....

....

Gallo White Zinfandel 2006

★ ★ ★

CALIFORNIA $8.95   (285767)

Like most white Zinfandels, this one lies on the sweeter side of the spectrum. It has fresh, bright flavours, while the texture is not too high in acid but is refreshing enough. Chill this down to bring out more acidity. It makes a pleasant sipping wine in the summer, or you can pair it with spicy food, like chicken in a barbecue sauce.

NOTES

....

....

....

....

....

Jeanjean Syrah Rosé 2007

★ ★ ★ ½

VIN DE PAYS D'OC, FRANCE $10.45   (355347)

The flavours and texture of rosés vary according to the red grape variety they're made from. This one, that uses Syrah, brims with vibrant flavours of fresh fruit. It's dry and medium bodied, with a crisp texture, and the acidity and fruit work very well together. It goes nicely with dishes that combine sweet and tart flavours, like roast turkey and cranberry sauce.

NOTES

....

....

....

....

....

Remy Pannier Rosé d'Anjou 2007

★ ★ ★

AOC ROSÉ D'ANJOU, FRANCE $10.95   (12641)

Anjou, in the Loire Valley, is renowned for its rosés. Most are made from the little-known variety Grolleau, but Cabernet and Gamay are becoming more common. This example delivers quite sweet flavours at first, but they're tamed by the crisp texture that makes this a versatile rosé for food. Serve it with spicy Asian dishes or with mixed appetizers. Or sip it by itself.

NOTES

....

....

....

....

....

Ted the Mule Grenache/Syrah 2006

★ ★ ★ ★

CÔTES DU RHÔNE, FRANCE $12.05   (622126)

This is one serious mule, but then I suspect mules are characteristically serious as well as stubborn. (The name is a play on *tête du mule*, meaning "stubborn," and future vintages will carry the French name.) Back to the wine, which is remarkably dense in flavour and texture, with a clean vibrancy to both. It's dry and medium bodied, and goes well with a spicy beef salad or with roast turkey and cranberries.

NOTES
....
....
....
....

Woodbridge White Zinfandel 2006

★ ★ ★ ½

CALIFORNIA $9.95   (249656)

White Zinfandel doesn't deserve its bad press. It's a favourite among Americans, but too many wine professionals (who should know better) sneer at it as being unworthy of serious consideration. This one is great for summer sipping or to pour with spicy foods, like chicken and ribs with zesty barbecue sauce. The bright flavours tame the sauce, and its crispness keeps your palate fresh. But why isn't it under a screw cap?

NOTES
....
....
....
....

Yellow Tail Rosé 2007

★ ★ ★ ½

SOUTH EASTERN AUSTRALIA $10.90   (37606)

The thing about the wallaby's tail on the Yellow Tail label is that it isn't yellow. Thereby hangs a tale, I'm sure. But it does have some pink, so there's a sort of authenticity to this wine. It's very pleasant for sipping in the summer (or in the winter, to remind you of summer), and has semi-sweet and bright flavours, and a fairly refreshing texture. It's also a candidate for spicy salads and appetizers.

NOTES
....
....
....
....

KOSHER WINE

TO BE CERTIFIED "KOSHER," wine must be made according to
rules that make it suitable for consumption by observant Jews. In
the past, most kosher wine was sweet, but modern kosher wine is
indistinguishable in flavour and texture from non-kosher wine.

Dalton 'Safsufa Vineyards' Cabernet Sauvignon 2006

★ ★ ★ ½

UPPER GALILEE, ISRAEL $16.10   (28266)

This is a flavour-filled Cabernet that has good complexity and a lively and tangy texture. Dry with moderate tannins, it's a good example of the new kosher wines that are indistinguishable in style and character from non-kosher varieties. This one goes well with brisket or with baked chicken breast and sautéed mushrooms.

NOTES

....

....

....

....

....

Don Mendoza Reserve Merlot 2006

★ ★ ★ ★

MENDOZA, ARGENTINA $10.50   (29306)

This is a really lovely Merlot at an excellent price. What's immediately striking is the refreshing quality of the texture. It's dry and delivers quite concentrated flavours, but it's raised above the fuller, fruitier style that's common at this price, and it comes across as light and fresh. Medium-bodied and lightly tannic, this goes well with braised or roasted red meats.

NOTES

....

....

....

....

....

Welnerberg Cabernet Sauvignon 2005

★ ★ ★ ½

WO SWARTLAND, SOUTH AFRICA $10.35   (28407)

Although this doesn't have a lot of Cabernet character, it's a well-made red that goes nicely with a wide variety of dishes. The flavours are vibrant, fresh, and concentrated, and it has a refreshing, lively texture that's friendly to food, whether you're eating chicken or beef. Medium-weight and dry, it has moderate tannins.

NOTES

....

....

....

....

....

Welnerberg Pinotage 2005

★ ★ ★

WO SWARTLAND, SOUTH AFRICA $10.65   (28423)

Pinotage is South Africa's signature red grape variety, and makes a full-flavoured red. Swartland is among South Africa's warmest wine regions. Combine the two and you get an intensely fruity, almost jammy, red, with a dense texture. It's dry and smooth, and goes well with beef ribs in barbecue sauce.

NOTES

....

....

....

....

....

SPARKLING WINE
& CHAMPAGNE

THERE'S THIS DIFFERENCE between Champagne and sparkling wine: All Champagnes are sparkling wines, but not all sparkling wines are Champagnes. Champagne is a sparkling wine made in the Champagne region of France, from specified grape varieties and in a method defined by wine law. Sparkling wines made elsewhere (even if from the same grape varieties and using the same method) cannot be called Champagne.

In this list, the sparkling wines are reviewed first, followed by the Champagnes.

SPARKLING WINE

★ ★ ★

Antonini Ceresa Prosecco La Robínía Extra Dry

ITALY $11.36   (593855)

[Non-vintage] Although many people think Prosecco is a style of wine, it's a grape variety used to make sparkling wine in the northeastern corner of Italy. It tends to be off-dry, like this example, which is fruity and easy drinking. It's ideal for sipping before a meal, but you can also serve it with spicy food, as the sparkling fruitiness will help tone down the heat.

NOTES

....

....

....

....

★ ★ ★ ½

Banrock Station Sparkling Chardonnay

AUSTRALIA $12.80   (534974)

[Non-vintage] This is another reliable, non-vintage sparkler that you'll find very versatile. It's the sort of wine you should keep in the fridge for emergencies, like a hard day, a Sunday, or an evening. Fruity flavoured, this tastes very good by itself or with appetizers or main courses. It goes as well with spicy Asian (Thai or Indian) food as with the barbecued chicken from the supermarket.

NOTES

....

....

....

....

★ ★ ★ ½

Bottega 'Il Vino dei Poeti' Prosecco Brut

ITALY $15.35   (897702)

[Non-vintage] Prosecco is a grape variety grown especially in the Veneto region of Italy, where it makes good-quality sparkling wine. Bottega is one of the prime producers, and you'll easily recognize this wine by its black and gold label. The wine inside is easy drinking and fruity, with just a hint of sweetness. It's crisp and clean in texture, leaves your palate feeling refreshed, and is ideal as an aperitif or with spicy appetizers.

NOTES

....

....

....

Bottega 'Petalo Il Vino Dell' Amore' Moscato

★ ★ ★

ITALY $14.15   (588780)

[Non-vintage] This slightly sweet and spicy sparkling wine might well reflect your evening or your partner (although I advise leaving the "slightly" out of your description). Chilled down, this makes a very pleasant wine for sipping, but you could also pair it with spicy appetizers. The flavours are easygoing, the texture crisp, and the mousse (the foam in your mouth) is soft and fruit filled.

NOTES

....

....

....

....

Château de Montgueret Crémant de Loire Brut

★ ★ ★ ★

FRANCE $20.45   (621896)

[Non-vintage] This sparkling wine is made in the same way as Champagne. It's a lovely blend of Chenin Blanc, Chardonnay, and Cabernet Franc. Slightly off-dry, with attractive and complex flavours, it's an excellent aperitif that will perk up your appetite. Alternatively, pair it with spicy Asian dishes or with zippy seafood such as garlic-ginger shrimp.

NOTES

....

....

....

....

Codorníu Brut Classico Cava

★ ★ ★ ★

SPAIN $12.10   (6262)

[Non-vintage] Cava is made in the same way as Champagne, which is to say that it goes through a fermentation in the bottle you buy (rather than being bottled after the fermentation is complete). This is a very attractive Cava, with great flavours and a lovely crisp and balanced texture. It has plenty of small bubbles and a soft mousse. Sip it alone or serve it with spicy chicken, pork, or seafood.

NOTES

....

....

....

Cora Gran Vino Spumante

★ ★ ★

ITALY $8.40   (17301)

[Non-vintage] This is an inexpensive sparkling wine that's as versatile as you want to make it. It has a moderate level of sweetness that's toned down by its acidity and the prickly feel of the bubbles. You can sip it by itself, serve it with spicy appetizers or main courses, or use it for fruit-based drinks, like mimosas.

NOTES

....

....

....

....

....

Freixenet 'Brut de Noirs' Cava Brut

★ ★ ★

SPAIN $12.85   (352369)

[Non-vintage] This is a rosé sparkling wine that makes a pretty addition to a summer table, and it's a reminder during winter that summer will return. It has bright, ripe, and sweet fruit flavours, but the wine itself is bone dry. The texture is crisp and refreshing, and the bubbles are plentiful and create a lovely mousse. This is perfect with a summer salad, but you can also serve it with baked ham or with roast chicken.

NOTES

....

....

....

....

Freixenet 'Carta Nevada' Cava Brut

★ ★ ★

SPAIN $11.95   (74757)

[Non-vintage] This is a Cava, made in the same way as Champagne, but from different grapes. Here, it's a three-way blend of Spain's native Parellada, Macabeo, and Xarel.lo varieties. The flavours here are concentrated, vibrant, and fresh, and it has quite good weight. It's crisp and lively in texture, with a decent crowd of bubbles. You can drink this as an aperitif or with spicy chicken or pork dishes.

NOTES

....

....

....

....

Freixenet 'Cordon Negro' Cava Brut

★ ★ ★ ★

SPAIN $13.45   (88591)

[Non-vintage] This is one of those reliable, versatile sparkling wines that you can count on. A blend of three grape varieties indigenous to Spain, and made in the same way as Champagne (the wine was fermented in the bottle you buy), it delivers lovely vibrant fruit flavours and has a zesty and refreshing texture. With all the fizz you want for a special occasion, serve it as an aperitif or with a spicy Asian dish.

NOTES

Hungaria 'Grande Cuvée' Brut

★ ★ ★ ½

HUNGARY $11.10   (619288)

[Non-vintage] Not only is this a good-quality sparkling wine, it's also socially responsible. It's the first sparkler I've seen that carries a warning to point the bottle away from people when you're opening it, in case the cork flies into someone's eye. The flavours are fruity, the texture is crisp and zesty, and the bubbles are fine. It's great as an aperitif or served with spicy seafood, chicken, or pork dishes.

NOTES

Navarro Correas Extra Brut

★ ★ ★

MENDOZA, ARGENTINA $15.95   (66563)

[Non-vintage] This is a very dry sparkling wine that has a lighter fizz than many, but is nonetheless quite attractive—as is its elegantly shaped bottle. The fruit flavours are delicate and nuanced, and the texture is quite zesty, allowing it to go well with food like smoked salmon or meat dishes with cream-based sauces.

NOTES

★ ★ ★

Seaview Sparkling Brut

AUSTRALIA $12.95   (216333)

[Non-vintage] This is the sort of versatile sparkling wine you need to have
on hand in case of emergencies or unexpected visitors, or to open after
a particularly bad day at work. It's dry, with a clean and crisp texture,
and it has quite well-defined fruit flavours. If you didn't drink it during
the week, serve it to guests on the weekend or match it with spicy pork,
chicken, seafood, or cream-based dishes. I said it was versatile.

NOTES

....

....

....

★ ★ ★ ½

Seaview Sparkling Shiraz

SOUTH EASTERN AUSTRALIA $14.95   (644054)

[Non-vintage] Some people shrink at the thought of drinking Australian
Shiraz *with bubbles*. Then there are others, like me, who love it. If you
haven't tried it, think of an Australian Shiraz, then think of sparkling
wine, then blend the thoughts. Better still, try the bloody wine. This
Seaview version gives you rich, intense fruit flavours with a crisp texture.
Serve it with spicy beef or pork dishes.

NOTES

....

....

....

★ ★ ★ ½

Segura Viudas Brut Reserva Cava

SPAIN $14.95   (158493)

[Non-vintage] "Cava" (which means "cellar") indicates that this is a sparkling wine made in Spain, using the same method (but usually different
grape varieties) that produces Champagne. It's a well-balanced wine with
solid fruit flavours, a crisp and tangy texture, nice mousse, and plenty of
quite small bubbles. It goes down very well with spicy Asian cuisine.

NOTES

....

....

....

....

Trius Brut
★ ★ ★ ★

NIAGARA PENINSULA, ONTARIO $24.95   (451641)

[Non-vintage] This Niagara sparkling wine is made from Chardonnay and Pinot Noir grapes and is fermented according to the method used for Champagne (what is now often called the "classic" or "traditional" method). It's a very well-balanced wine, with lovely, defined fruit flavours complemented by a clean and crisp texture. The mousse is soft, the bubbles small, and it's an excellent party or aperitif sparkler.

NOTES

Wolf Blass 'Yellow Label' Sparkling Brut
★ ★ ★ ½

SOUTH EASTERN AUSTRALIA $16.85   (649996)

[Non-vintage] This is another of those well-made, good-value, versatile sparkling wines that you can sip alone, mix with orange or other juice, or drink with appetizers or main courses. The secret is in the balance—and you have it here—between good solid fruit flavours and crisp, refreshing texture. If you're planning to drink this with food, think of fairly rich chicken, pork, or turkey dishes.

NOTES

CHAMPAGNE

★ ★ ★ ★   **Lanson 'Black Label'**

AOC CHAMPAGNE $49.95   (41889)

[Non-vintage] This is a delightfully complex Champagne at the less expensive end of the price spectrum. The flavours are well defined and it's crisp and clean, with a soft mousse (the froth that forms in your mouth). Look at the bubbles in your glass and you'll see they're small and form vertical lines, both signs of a good-quality Champagne. Drink this as an aperitif or with appetizers.

NOTES

★ ★ ★ ★   **Moët et Chandon Champagne Brut Impérial**

AOC CHAMPAGNE $65.90   (453084)

[Non-vintage] Moët et Chandon is the largest of the Champagne houses, producing about 25 million bottles a year. That means there's almost enough for one bottle of their Champagne to be opened every second. Once you've poured a glass, you'll see the lines of tiny bubbles and taste delicate fruit flavours. Medium-bodied and with a gentle mousse, this makes an excellent Champagne to serve at parties.

NOTES

★ ★ ★ ★   **Mumm Cordon Rouge Champagne Brut**

AOC CHAMPAGNE $59.45   (308056)

[Non-vintage] You could serve this on Mother's Day, but the Mumm here is pronounced "moom," to rhyme with "moon." It's one of the best-known Champagnes and you can't miss it on the shelf in the LCBO; it's the one with the diagonal red stripe (the "cordon rouge"). It's just well made, with all the crispness you want from Champagne, not to mention the nuanced flavours. With a soft mousse and good weight, it's a great complement to chicken, turkey, or rich fish dishes.

NOTES

★ ★ ★ ★

Nicolas Feuillatte 'Réserve Particulière'

AOC CHAMPAGNE $51.35   (537605)

[Non-vintage] This is a really attractive Champagne from start to finish. Pour it and watch the streams of small bubbles—always considered a sign of quality in a sparkling wine—then sip it and appreciate the zestiness of the first mouthful and the creamy mousse it forms. The flavours are well defined and have the complexity you want in a Champagne. This makes an excellent aperitif, but it also carries through to the table and would go with rich chicken dishes.

NOTES

★ ★ ★ ★

Pol Roger 'Extra Cuvée de Réserve' Brut

AOC CHAMPAGNE $57.10   (51953)

[Non-vintage] This is a very good quality Champagne at a very good price. It has everything you want: fine fruit flavours with some complexity, a crisp and zesty texture, lots of tiny bubbles streaming up from the bottom of the glass, and a prickly but not too harsh mousse in the mouth. It's ideal as an aperitif, but you can carry it to the table, too, where it goes well with spicy seafood or chicken dishes.

NOTES

★ ★ ★ ★

Veuve Clicquot-Ponsardin Brut

AOC CHAMPAGNE $69.45   (563338)

[Non-vintage] Named for the woman who not only took over production but improved it after her Champagne-producer husband died, this has become an iconic sparkling wine. The stylish orange label stands out on the shelf. The Champagne itself is a byword for balance, with well-defined flavours, a crisp, refreshing texture, and fine bubbles and mousse. You can drink this on its own or serve it with smoked salmon, or chicken or pork in a cream sauce.

NOTES

SWEET &
DESSERT WINE

ALL DESSERT WINES ARE SWEET, but not all sweet wines are suitable for dessert. For example, icewine, which is a style Ontario is famous for, is often too saccharine for desserts but goes well with foie gras (which is normally served as an appetizer or as part of a main course) and blue cheese. This list includes a number of sweet wines, and I've suggested food matches for each.

★ ★ ★ ★ ½

Cave Spring 'Indian Summer' Select Late Harvest Riesling 2006

VQA NIAGARA PENINSULA $24.95   (415901)

[375 mL] This is not icewine, although the grapes were partly frozen when picked. They were left on the vine past the usual harvest date to shrivel and lose water, then picked after the first frost. The result is a wine with sweet, but not very sweet, flavours that are complex and delicious, complemented by brisk acidity. It's lovely to drink by itself, but you can serve it (chilled) with any fruit-based dessert that's no sweeter than the wine.

NOTES

....

....

....

....

★ ★ ★ ★ ★

Henry of Pelham Riesling Icewine 2006

VQA NIAGARA PENINSULA $54.95   (430561)

[Vintages Essential, 375 mL] This is an icewine that delivers the best in the style. It has all the sweetness that shrivelled, frozen grapes can put out, but it's nuanced and layered. Meanwhile, the threat of a cloying, teeth-hurting experience is averted by the nice line of acidity. It's a more drinkable icewine than many, and for this reason you could chill it slightly (10 to 15 minutes in the fridge), then sip it by itself or drink it with foie gras.

NOTES

....

....

....

....

★ ★ ★ ★

Jackson-Triggs Proprietors' Reserve Vidal Icewine 2006

VQA NIAGARA PENINSULA $45.95   (594010)

[Vintages Essential, 375 mL] Icewine is now made from a wide range of grape varieties—including red—and there are also sparkling icewines. But the majority are made from Riesling and Vidal. This Vidal is sweet, to be sure (and icewine couldn't be anything else), but it's fruity and fairly light on its feet for a medium- to full-bodied wine. The acidity is clean and balancing, and you can drink this with not-too-sweet fruit desserts or blue cheese.

NOTES

....

....

....

Lakeview Cellars Vidal Icewine 2006

★★★ ½

VQA NIAGARA PENINSULA $19.95   (522672)

[Vintages Essential, 200 mL] The 200 mL bottle is an excellent size (about half the volume of a normal bottle of icewine), serving four to six people comfortably. And they'll enjoy this rich example. It's full bodied and packed with luscious, opulent flavours. But it has the necessary seam of acidity in the texture that tames the sweetness. Chill it and drink it alone or with orange-infused crème brûlée.

NOTES

....

....

....

....

....

Pelee Island Late Harvest Vidal 2007

★★★

VQA ONTARIO $11.85   (594184)

This is a simple, straightforward semi-sweet white that's very appealing. It delivers solid fruit flavours with a little complexity, and a texture that's mouth filling, smooth, and quite refreshing. Overall, it's a good effort and the crispness ensures that the flavours aren't too sweet. You can chill it down and sip it alone or drink it with spicy Asian dishes or with blue cheese.

NOTES

....

....

....

....

....

PORT

PORT IS A SWEET, FORTIFIED WINE (usually red, sometimes white) made in the Douro region of Portugal. It's generally served after dinner with dessert, cheese, nuts, or on its own, and some people like the combination of port and a cigar. Although other countries produce fortified wines that are sometimes labelled "port," the name is properly reserved for the wine produced in the Douro region according to the rules set out for port producers there.

Ferreira 'Dona Antonia Reserve' Port

★ ★ ★ ★ ½

DOC PORTO $19.00   (157586)

Named for the head of the Ferreira port-producing family in the early 19th century, this is a luscious port. It delivers sweet, rich, and multi-layered flavours, and a texture that's quite viscous and seems to swell in your mouth. But the acidity kicks in and kills the sweetness, leaving you with a fruity and complex finish. It's delicious on its own or with blue cheese and roasted nuts.

NOTES

....

....

....

....

Kopke Fine Ruby Port

★ ★ ★ ★

DOC PORTO $14.20   (35766)

The British long dominated the port industry, and England was for centuries the main market for the wine. Kopke is from one of the few port houses actually owned by a Portuguese family. Their ruby port is sweet and rich but it has a tangy texture that cuts through the sweetness. You can sip it on its own or drink it with the usual port pairings, such as blue cheese.

NOTES

....

....

....

....

Paarl 'Vintage Character' Cape Ruby

★ ★ ★

SOUTH AFRICA $9.75   (28951)

Many New World countries (Australia, New Zealand, and South Africa) produced masses of fortified wine before they were able to turn out quality table wine. Not strictly a port, this fortified wine is remarkably port-like. It has rich, sweet, fruity flavours, a tangy texture, and some tannic structure that leaves your mouth sweet but dry. Sip it slightly chilled or drink it with fruit cake.

NOTES

....

....

....

....

Taylor Fladgate 'First Estate' Reserve Port
★ ★ ★ ★ ½

DOC PORTO $15.60   (309401)

This is made in a slightly less-sweet style than most ports. There are some red wines described as port-like because they're so rich, intense, and sweet, and if you think of those, this port is just across the line, in a style approaching red wine. Being less sweet, it's easier drinking and goes well with aged cheeses (like very old, crumbly cheddar). The texture here is intense and rich, but it leaves a drying sensation in your mouth.

NOTES
....
....
....
....

Taylor Fladgate Late Bottled Vintage Port (Bottled 2002)
★ ★ ★ ★

DOC PORTO $17.95   (46946)

As the name suggests, Late Bottled Vintage (LBV) ports are aged in barrels for a minimum specified period before being bottled and sold. This LBV delivers complex sweet flavours, but the tangy texture has enough acid bite so that it cuts through the sweetness and prevents it from being cloying. This is a port that goes well with rich fruitcake or blue cheese.

NOTES
....
....
....
....

Warre's 'Otima' 10-Year-Old Port
★ ★ ★ ★

DOC PORTO $22.85   (566174)

[500 mL] If you think of port as an after-dinner drink with the colour and weight of the leather armchairs containing the crusty old guys who sip it, try Otima. It still has lovely sweet fruit flavours but it's made with a lighter texture—as you might expect from the colour of this port, which is paler than most. You can chill it as an aperitif or drink it at room temperature after dinner.

NOTES
....
....
....
....

SHERRY

SHERRY IS A FORTIFIED WINE made in Jerez, a wine region in the south of Spain. It comes in many styles, from clear, crisp, light, and dry, to black, heavy, viscous, and sweet. You'll find other fortified wines labelled sherry, but only fortified wine from the Jerez region made in a designated way can properly be called sherry.

Alvear's Fino Montilla

★★★ ½

DO MONTILLA $10.95   (112771)

[Non-vintage] This isn't sherry, as it isn't made in Jerez, in southern Spain. But, Montilla, the region next to Jerez, produces wines in the same styles as sherry, from delicate and bone dry to rich and sweet. This Fino Montilla is on the delicate and dry end of the spectrum. It's crisp and refreshing, with a light body, and goes well with salty Spanish tapas, like olives and grilled octopus.

NOTES

....

....

....

....

Croft Original Fine Pale Cream Sherry

★★★ ½

DO JEREZ $15.25   (73452)

[Non-vintage] This is a fairly sweet style (it's a dry fino sherry that's been sweetened), rather like a late-harvest wine. It has the classic, complex, pungent sherry flavours, but it's fairly light and you can drink it as a dessert wine. Chill it down a little (put a full bottle in the fridge for 20 to 30 minutes) then serve it with a fruit-based dessert that's not too sweet.

NOTES

....

....

....

....

Harvey's Bristol Cream Sherry

★★★★

DO JEREZ $19.00   (215509)

[Non-vintage] Some people think of sweet sherry as an old-timers' drink, the sort of thing your grandmother might sip a few clandestine glasses of during the evening. But Harvey's Bristol Cream is a delicious, lightly viscous blend that displays many appealing flavours. You can sip it with crème caramel or drink it as a summer aperitif—on the rocks with a slice of orange.

NOTES

....

....

....

....

Osborne Santa Maria Cream Sherry

★ ★ ★ ½

DO JEREZ $11.25   (31120)

[Non-vintage] Sherry comes in many styles and with many names—too many for the average consumer to worry about. "Cream" sherries like this one tend to be richer and sweeter and are often best sipped on their own, although you can drink them with desserts (as long as the dessert is no sweeter than the sherry). This one delivers a real range of sweet and pungent flavours but has enough bite that it doesn't become cloying.

NOTES

....

....

....

....

....

INDEX

INDEX

This index includes the main styles (such as Amarone), grape varieties, and blends, and well-known regions (such as Beaujolais and Chianti) that define their wines. For the most part, grape varieties and blends are indexed only when they are declared on the main label.

ABOUT THE AUTHOR

ROD PHILLIPS writes a weekly wine column for the *Ottawa Citizen* and contributes to wine magazines, podcasts, and other wine media in Canada, the US, and Europe. Among the magazines he has written for are *World of Fine Wine, Vines, Wine Access,* and *Wine Spectator.* Apart from *The 500 Best-Value Wines in the LCBO,* he has written two other books on wine, judges in wine competitions in Canada and Europe, has talked about wine on the CBC, and gives wine classes. He was the curator of an exhibition on the history of Canadian wine at the Museum of Civilization in 2004/2005, and was named "Wine Journalist of the Year" at the 2007 Ontario Wine Awards. He regularly visits wine regions and wineries around the world.

Rod publishes *Winepointer,* a bi-weekly electronic newsletter, which reviews LCBO, Vintages, and other wines available in Ontario, and *Worlds of Wine,* a monthly electronic newsletter that features articles on wine. You can subscribe free at www.rodphillipsonwine.com. Contact Rod at rod@rodphillipsonwine.com.